W9-AXZ-026

SERIES

JUN -- 2011

Urban America

Other Books of Related Interest:

Opposing Viewpoints Series

Domestic Violence

Interracial America

Street Teens

Welfare

Current Controversies Series

Family Violence

Illegal Immigration

The Uninsured

At Issue Series

Green Cities

How Can the Poor Be Helped?

Should the United States Be Multilingual?

"Congress shall make
no law ... abridging
the freedom of speech,
or of the press."

First Amendment to the US Constitution

The basic foundation of our democracy is the First Amendment guarantee of freedom of expression. The Opposing Viewpoints Series is dedicated to the concept of this basic freedom and the idea that it is more important to practice it than to enshrine it.

OPPOSING VIEWPOINTS® SERIES

Urban America

Roman Espejo, Book Editor

GREENHAVEN PRESS
A part of Gale, Cengage Learning

GALE
CENGAGE Learning

Detroit • New York • San Francisco • New Haven, Conn • Waterville, Maine • London

Christine Nasso, *Publisher*
Elizabeth Des Chenes, *Managing Editor*

© 2011 Greenhaven Press, a part of Gale, Cengage Learning

Gale and Greenhaven Press are registered trademarks used herein under license.

For more information, contact:
Greenhaven Press
27500 Drake Rd.
Farmington Hills, MI 48331-3535
Or you can visit our Internet site at gale.cengage.com

For product information and technology assistance, contact us at

Gale Customer Support, 1-800-877-4253
For permission to use material from this text or product, submit all requests online at www.cengage.com/permissions

Further permissions questions can be emailed to permissionrequest@cengage.com

Articles in Greenhaven Press anthologies are often edited for length to meet page requirements. In addition, original titles of these works are changed to clearly present the main thesis and to explicitly indicate the author's opinion. Every effort is made to ensure that Greenhaven Press accurately reflects the original intent of the authors. Every effort has been made to trace the owners of copyrighted material.

Cover image © Janine Wiedel Photolibrary/Alamy.

LIBRARY OF CONGRESS CATALOGING-IN-PUBLICATION DATA

Urban America / Roman Espejo, book editor.
    p. cm. -- (Opposing viewpoints)
    Includes bibliographical references and index.
    ISBN 978-0-7377-5249-6 (hardcover) -- ISBN 978-0-7377-5250-2 (pbk.)
    1. Cities and towns--United States--Juvenile literature. 2. Urbanization--United States--Juvenile literature. 3. Social problems--United States--Juvenile literature. 4. Crime--United States--Juvenile literature. I. Espejo, Roman, 1977-
    HT123.U717 2011
    307.760973--dc22

                                                                    2010047519

Printed in the United States of America
1 2 3 4 5 6 7 15 14 13 12 11

Contents

Chapter 3: How Can the Lives of Urban Children Be Improved?

Chapter 4: What Is the Future of Urban America?

Why Consider Opposing Viewpoints?

> *"The only way in which a human being can make some approach to knowing the whole of a subject is by hearing what can be said about it by persons of every variety of opinion and studying all modes in which it can be looked at by every character of mind. No wise man ever acquired his wisdom in any mode but this."*
>
> *John Stuart Mill*

In our media-intensive culture it is not difficult to find differing opinions. Thousands of newspapers and magazines and dozens of radio and television talk shows resound with differing points of view. The difficulty lies in deciding which opinion to agree with and which "experts" seem the most credible. The more inundated we become with differing opinions and claims, the more essential it is to hone critical reading and thinking skills to evaluate these ideas. Opposing Viewpoints books address this problem directly by presenting stimulating debates that can be used to enhance and teach these skills. The varied opinions contained in each book examine many different aspects of a single issue. While examining these conveniently edited opposing views, readers can develop critical thinking skills such as the ability to compare and contrast authors' credibility, facts, argumentation styles, use of persuasive techniques, and other stylistic tools. In short, the Opposing Viewpoints Series is an ideal way to attain the higher-level thinking and reading skills so essential in a culture of diverse and contradictory opinions.

In addition to providing a tool for critical thinking, *Opposing Viewpoints* books challenge readers to question their own strongly held opinions and assumptions. Most people form their opinions on the basis of upbringing, peer pressure, and personal, cultural, or professional bias. By reading carefully balanced opposing views, readers must directly confront new ideas as well as the opinions of those with whom they disagree. This is not to argue simplistically that everyone who reads opposing views will—or should—change his or her opinion. Instead, the series enhances readers' understanding of their own views by encouraging confrontation with opposing ideas. Careful examination of others' views can lead to the readers' understanding of the logical inconsistencies in their own opinions, perspective on why they hold an opinion, and the consideration of the possibility that their opinion requires further evaluation.

Evaluating Other Opinions

To ensure that this type of examination occurs, *Opposing Viewpoints* books present all types of opinions. Prominent spokespeople on different sides of each issue as well as well-known professionals from many disciplines challenge the reader. An additional goal of the series is to provide a forum for other, less known, or even unpopular viewpoints. The opinion of an ordinary person who has had to make the decision to cut off life support from a terminally ill relative, for example, may be just as valuable and provide just as much insight as a medical ethicist's professional opinion. The editors have two additional purposes in including these less known views. One, the editors encourage readers to respect others' opinions—even when not enhanced by professional credibility. It is only by reading or listening to and objectively evaluating others' ideas that one can determine whether they are worthy of consideration. Two, the inclusion of such viewpoints encourages the important critical thinking skill of objectively evaluating an author's credentials and bias. This evaluation will illuminate an author's reasons for taking a particular stance on an issue and will aid in readers' evaluation of the author's ideas.

It is our hope that these books will give readers a deeper understanding of the issues debated and an appreciation of the complexity of even seemingly simple issues when good and honest people disagree. This awareness is particularly important in a democratic society such as ours in which people enter into public debate to determine the common good. Those with whom one disagrees should not be regarded as enemies but rather as people whose views deserve careful examination and may shed light on one's own.

Thomas Jefferson once said that "difference of opinion leads to inquiry, and inquiry to truth." Jefferson, a broadly educated man, argued that "if a nation expects to be ignorant and free . . . it expects what never was and never will be." As individuals and as a nation, it is imperative that we consider the opinions of others and examine them with skill and discernment. The *Opposing Viewpoints* Series is intended to help readers achieve this goal.

David L. Bender and Bruno Leone,
Founders

Introduction

"*[The High Line] offers a hopeful model for industrial reuse for other cities around the world.*"

—*Friends of the High Line*

"*I prefer to give to a soup kitchen than pay for artfully arranged grass.*"

—*Maya Hess,*
New York City resident

In June 2009, New York mayor Michael Bloomberg cut the ribbon of the High Line in Manhattan, opening the first section of "the park in the sky" to the public. The elevated railway—rundown and overgrown with weeds, wild grasses, and trees—had been closed for nearly two decades and was scheduled to be demolished. The project is the brainchild of Joshua David and Robert Hammond, a writer and painter, respectively, who met at a community board meeting and shared a fascination with the structure. "I fell in love with the very thing most people were complaining about, this rusty eyesore from the city's industrial past," Hammond explains. He adds, "I saw this as a once-in-a-lifetime opportunity to preserve a mile and a half of Manhattan as an uninterrupted walkway and vantage point for people to enjoy on their own terms."[1]

Determined to save and rehabilitate the railway line, the duo established Friends of the High Line in 1999. They were not the first to try, however. "Of course, we didn't realize we were stepping into a fight that had been in the courts since the early '80s," David admits.[2] The nonprofit organization

1. Quoted in *New York Times*, July 11, 2008.
2. Quoted in *New York Magazine*, April 29, 2007.

held a benefit to raise the $60,000 in legal fees to stop the demolition of the High Line, gained the support of celebrities and prominent residents, and secured the cooperation of the Bloomberg administration, which earmarked funds for the project in 2004. In addition, Friends of the High Line brought in $44 million for its completion; the first and second sections cost $152 million.

As of September 2010, the open section of the High Line stretched from Gansevoort Street to Twentieth Street, with the second section scheduled to open in the fall of 2011. With its more than two hundred species of plants, its wooden deck chairs, and its expansive views of Manhattan and the Hudson River, the park has quickly become a celebrated icon of a new kind of urban renewal. Jill Fehrenbacher, founder of the green design blog Inhabitat, says the "High Line exemplifies effective adaptive urban reuse in a city that is littered with structures and spaces that have since reached the end of their useful life."[3] Indeed, the park was created with the environment in mind. "One could boast that there's going to be some carbon reduction with the amount of greenery that we've brought there," claims James Corner, landscape architect of the High Line. He adds, "All the materials are recyclable or come from sustainable sources, so there's nothing here that's ostentatious or out of place."[4] And the High Line has attracted businesses and developers to the neighborhood. It is the location of the Standard, a new luxury boutique hotel, and dozens of projects are in construction or development in the area, including a branch of the Whitney Museum of American Art. Mayor Bloomberg hails the High Line as "an extraordinary gift to our city's future" that "lives up to its highest expectations."[5]

3. Inhabitat, August 23, 2010. http://inhabitat.com/2010/08/23/interview-architect-james-corner-on-the-design-of-high-line/.
4. Quoted in Inhabitat, August 23, 2010.
5. Quoted in New York Times, June 9, 2009. www.nytimes.com/2009/06/09/arts/design/09highline-RO.html.

Still, the slice of urban paradise also became a point of contention. When Friends of the High Line sought backing for its proposed improvement district after the park opened—which would tax nearby property owners to cover maintenance costs—businesses cried foul, including some of Chelsea's independent art galleries. "You're asking a very small community to support in perpetuity the High Line. It's like telling people on the East Side and the West Side to support Central Park,"[6] contended Tara Reddi, a gallery director and board president of Chelsea Arts Tower. In addition, residents worry about keeping the neighborhood's character intact in the face of rising costs. "The greatest value in my life is not that the value of my property goes up," argued Joshua Mack, who started a petition against the improvement district with another property owner. "There are other things that I'm concerned about—one of them is diversity."[7] In response to such objections, Friends of the High Line placed the proposal on hold, stating that "many strongly supported the concept."[8]

Many tout the High Line as a success story for preservation efforts and green development. But others anticipate that it may diminish affordable housing, small businesses, and local cultures that distinguish the surrounding neighborhood. *Opposing Viewpoints: Urban America* investigates these and other urban concerns in the following chapters: What Problems Are Faced by Urban America? What Government Programs Would Improve Urban America? How Can the Lives of Urban Children Be Improved? and What Is the Future of Urban America? The authors of the viewpoints debate the state and prospects of the nation's cities.

6. Quoted in *Villager*, August 12–18, 2009. www.thevillager.com/villager_328/highline plans.html.
7. Quoted in *Villager*, August 12–18, 2009.
8. Quoted in *Curbed NY*, August 21, 2009. http://ny.curbed.com/archives/2009/08/21/ high_line_scraps_derided_high_line_improvement_district.php.

OPPOSING
VIEWPOINTS®
SERIES

CHAPTER 1

What Problems Are Faced by Urban America?

Chapter Preface

Many health experts and organizations claim America's inner-city children suffer disproportionately from asthma compared with other groups. The Arizona Respiratory Center (ARC) identifies poverty and living conditions as causes of increased asthma among urban children. "Among poor inner-city children, asthma is more severe and less likely to receive the consistent, long-term medical treatment that more affluent families can maintain," ARC states on its website. "Plus, because inner-city children tend to spend more time indoors than other children, certain indoor allergens—especially cockroaches, dust mites, pets, and mold—can greatly increase their asthma symptoms."[1] Others suggest that harmful environmental factors in urban areas contribute to higher rates of the disease. "The combination of air pollutants, aeroallergens, heat waves, and unhealthy air masses . . . causes damage to the respiratory systems, particularly for growing children, and these impacts disproportionately affect poor and minority groups in the inner cities,"[2] maintains the Center for Health and the Global Environment at the Harvard Medical School.

Programs have been launched in response to the urban asthma epidemic. In New York City, the Childhood Asthma Initiative ran a campaign with the slogan, "I have asthma, but asthma doesn't have me," from 1997 to 2001. During those years, pediatric hospitalizations for asthma dropped more than 30 percent. In Connecticut, the Breathe Easy Program, which instructs health care workers on how to better diagnose the disease in children, reduced the number of asthma-related visits to hospitals and emergency rooms. And in Baltimore, the Community Asthma Program and the Center for Reduc-

1. www.arc.arizona.edu, www.arc.arizona.edu/research/inner-city-asthma-study.html.
2. Medical News Service, May 8, 2004. www.medicalnewsservice.com/fullstory.cfm ?storyID=2257.

ing Asthma Disparities teach families how to manage the disease, from helping to secure medications to distributing supplies to reduce allergens in the home. "Several city-based or regional asthma intervention programs have had significant success,"[3] says Aliyah Baruchin, an investigative reporter. The authors of the viewpoints in the following chapter debate various other issues and challenges facing urban America in the early twenty-first century.

3. *New York Times*, August 30, 2007. http://health.nytimes.com/ref/health/healthguide/esn-asthmachildren-ess.html.

> "Don't tell me there's no role for govern-
> ment in lifting up our cities [out of
> poverty]."

The Government Can Help End the Cycle of Urban Poverty

Barack Obama

Barack Obama is the forty-fourth president of the United States; he was a US senator from Illinois when he wrote the following viewpoint, in which he claims poverty endures in inner cities and that it particularly affects minorities. He asserts that African Americans in poor urban neighborhoods are likely to be trapped in a cycle of economic and familial instability, poor education, crime, and unemployment. Obama insists, however, that comprehensive government antipoverty programs can significantly improve the odds for these communities' next generation, and he urges more government and taxpayer support for such efforts.

As you read, consider the following questions:

1. As stated by the author, what is the scope of poverty in America?

Barack Obama, "Remarks of Senator Barack Obama: Changing the Odds for Urban America," July 18, 2007.

2. How does the Harlem Children's Zone serve poor urban families, according to Obama?

3. How does the author propose to help the working poor rise out of poverty?

It's been four decades since [Senator] Bobby Kennedy crouched in a shack along the Mississippi Delta and looked into the wide, listless eyes of a hungry child. Again and again he tried to talk to this child, but each time his efforts were met with only a blank stare of desperation. And when Kennedy turned to the reporters traveling with him, with tears in his eyes he asked a single question about poverty in America:

"How can a country like this allow it?"

Forty years later [in 2007], we're still asking that question. It echoes on the streets of Compton [California] and Detroit, and throughout the mining towns of West Virginia. It lingers with every image we see of the 9th Ward [of New Orleans] and the rural Gulf Coast, where poverty thrived long before [Hurricane] Katrina came ashore. . . .

Every American Is Vulnerable

The challenge is greater than it has been in generations, but that's all the more reason for this generation to act. One in every eight Americans now lives in poverty; a rate that has nearly doubled since 1980. That's an income of about $20,000 a year for a family of four. One in three Americans—one in every three—is now classified as low-income. That's $40,000 a year for a family of four.

Today's economy has made it easier to fall into poverty. The fall is often more precipitous and more permanent than ever before. You used to be able to find a good job without a degree from college or even high school. Today that's nearly impossible. You used to be able to count on your job to be there for your entire life. Today almost any job can be shipped overseas in an instant.

The jobs that remain are paying less and offering fewer benefits, as employers have succeeded in busting up unions and cutting back on health care and pensions to stay competitive with the companies abroad that are paying their workers next to nothing.

Every American is vulnerable to the insecurities and anxieties of this new economy. And that's why the single most important focus of my economic agenda as President will be to pursue policies that create jobs and make work pay.

This means investing in education from early childhood through college, so our workers are ready to compete with any workers for the best jobs the world has to offer. It means investing more in research, science, and technology so that those new jobs and those new industries are created right here in America. And while we can't stop every job from going overseas, we can stop giving tax breaks to the companies who send them there and start giving them to companies who create jobs at home.

We can also start making sure these jobs keep folks out of poverty. When I'm President, I will raise the minimum wage and make it a living wage by making sure that it rises every time the cost of living does. I'll start letting our unions do what they do best again—organize our workers and lift up our middle-class. And I'll finally make sure every American has affordable health care that stays with you no matter what happens by passing my plan to provide universal coverage and cut the cost of health care by up to $2500 per family.

All of these policies will give more families a chance to grab hold of the ladder to middle-class security, and they'll make the climb a little easier.

But poverty is not just a function of simple economics. It's also a matter of where you live. There are vast swaths of rural America and block after block in our cities where poverty is not just a crisis that hits pocketbooks, but a disease that infects every corner of the community. I will be outlining my rural agenda in the coming weeks, but today I want to talk about what we can do as a nation to combat the poverty that persists in our cities.

This kind of poverty is not an issue I just discovered for the purposes of a campaign; it is the cause that led me to a life of public service almost twenty-five years ago.

I was just two years out of college when I first moved to the South Side of Chicago to become a community organizer. I was hired by a group of churches that were trying to deal with steel plant closures that had devastated the surrounding neighborhoods. Everywhere you looked, businesses were boarded up and schools were crumbling and teenagers were standing aimlessly on street corners, without jobs and without hope.

Difficult to Escape

What's most overwhelming about urban poverty is that it's so difficult to escape—it's isolating and it's everywhere. If you are an African-American child unlucky enough to be born into one of these neighborhoods, you are most likely to start life hungry or malnourished. You are less likely to start with a father in your household, and if he is there, there's a fifty-fifty chance that he never finished high school and the same chance he doesn't have a job. Your school isn't likely to have the right books or the best teachers. You're more likely to encounter gang-activities than after-school activities. And if you can't find a job because the most successful businessman in your neighborhood is a drug dealer, you're more likely to join that gang yourself. Opportunity is scarce, role models are few, and there is little contact with the normalcy of life outside those streets.

What you learn when you spend your time in these neighborhoods trying to solve these problems is that there are no easy solutions and no perfect arguments. And you come to understand that for the last four decades, both ends of the political spectrum have been talking past one another.

It's true that there were many effective programs that emerged from [President] Lyndon Johnson's War on Poverty. But there were also some ineffective programs that were defended anyway, as well as an inability of some on the left to acknowledge that the problems of absent fathers or persistent crime were indeed problems that needed to be addressed.

The right has often seized on these failings as proof that the government can't and shouldn't do a thing about poverty—that it is a result of individual moral failings and cultural pathologies and so we should just sit back and let these cities fend for themselves. And so [President] Ronald Reagan launched his assault on welfare queens, and [President] George [W.] Bush spent the last six years [2001–2007] slashing programs to combat poverty, and job training, and substance abuse, and child abuse.

Well, we know that's not the answer. When you're in these neighborhoods, you can see what a difference it makes to have a government that cares. You can see what a free lunch program does for a hungry child. You can see what a little extra money from an earned income tax credit does for a family that's struggling. You can see what prenatal care does for the health of a mother and a newborn. So don't tell me there's no role for government in lifting up our cities.

But you can also see what a difference it makes when people start caring for themselves. It makes a difference when a father realizes that responsibility does not end at conception; when he understands that what makes you a man is not the ability to have a child but the courage to raise one. It makes a difference when a parent turns off the TV once in awhile, puts away the video games, and starts reading to their child, and getting involved in his education. It makes a difference when we realize that a child who shoots another child has a hole in his heart that no government can fill. That makes a difference.

So there are no easy answers and perfect arguments. As Dr. [Martin Luther] King [Jr.] said, it is not either-or, it is both-and. Hope is not found in any single ideology—an insistence on doing the same thing with the same result year after year.

Healing the Entire Community

Hope is found in what works. In those South Side neighborhoods, hope was found in the after school programs we created, and the job training programs we put together, and the organizing skills we taught residents so that they could stand up to a government that wasn't standing up for them. Hope is found here at THE ARC, where you've provided thousands of children with shelter from the streets and a home away from home. And if you travel a few hours north of here, you will find hope amid ninety-seven neighborhood blocks in the heart of Harlem.

This is the home of the Harlem Children's Zone—an all-encompassing, all-hands-on-deck anti-poverty effort that is literally saving a generation of children in a neighborhood where they were never supposed to have a chance.

The philosophy behind the project is simple—if poverty is a disease that infects an entire community in the form of unemployment and violence; failing schools and broken homes, then we can't just treat those symptoms in isolation. We have to heal that entire community. And we have to focus on what actually works.

If you're a child who's born in the Harlem Children's Zone, you start life differently than other inner-city children. Your parents probably went to what they call "Baby College", a place where they received counseling on how to care for newborns and what to expect in those first months. You start school right away, because there's early childhood education. When your parents are at work, you have a safe place to play and learn, because there's child care, and afterschool programs, even in the summer. There are innovative charter schools to attend. There's free medical services that offer care when you're sick and preventive services to stay healthy. There's affordable, good food available so you're not malnourished. There are job counselors and financial counselors. There's technology training and crime prevention.

You don't just sign up for this program; you're actively recruited for it, because the idea is that if everyone is involved, and no one slips through the cracks, then you really can change an entire community. Geoffrey Canada, the program's inspirational, innovative founder, put it best—instead of helping some kids beat the odds, the Harlem Children's Zone is actually changing the odds altogether.

And it's working. Parents in Harlem are actually reading more to their children. Their kids are staying in school and passing statewide tests at higher rates than other children in New York City. They're going to college in a place where it was once unheard of. They've even placed third at a national chess championship.

So we know this works. And if we know it works, there's no reason this program should stop at the end of those blocks in Harlem. It's time to change the odds for neighborhoods all across America. And that's why when I'm President, the first part of my plan to combat urban poverty will be to replicate the Harlem Children's Zone in twenty cities across the country. We'll train staff, we'll have them draw up detailed plans with attainable goals, and the federal government will provide half of the funding for each city, with the rest coming from philanthropies and businesses.

Now, how much will this cost? I'll be honest—it can't be done on the cheap. It will cost a few billion dollars a year. We won't just spend the money because we can—every step these

Detachment from the Mainstream Economy

The inner-city poor do lack human capital to a profound degree in comparison with other groups. They are segregated and detached from the labor market. Demand for their skills at manual labor has declined. They face discrimination in employment and housing. They live in a social milieu that reinforces detachment from the mainstream economy, though how much that milieu results in a different set of values and behaviors is subject to much debate. Similarly, segregation has separated the inner-city poor physically from employment opportunities, but there is no clear agreement about the impact of that separation.

Michael B. Teitz and Karen Chapple, Cityscape, *1998.*

cities take will be evaluated, and if certain plans or programs aren't working, we will stop them and try something else.

But we will find the money to do this because we can't afford not to. Dr. King once remarked that if we can find the money to put a man on the moon, then we can find the money to put a man on his own two feet. There's no reason we should be spending tens of thousands of dollars a year to imprison one of these kids when they turn eighteen when we could be spending $3,500 to turn their lives around with this program. And to really put it in perspective, think of it this way. The Harlem Children's Zone is saving a generation of children for $46 million a year. That's about what the war in Iraq costs American taxpayers every four hours.

So let's invest this money. Let's change the odds in urban America by focusing on what works.

Planning for Urban America

The second part of my plan will do this by providing families the support they need to raise their children. I'll pass the plan I outlined [in 2006] that will provide more financial support to fathers who make the responsible choice to help raise their children and crack down on the fathers who don't. And we'll help new mothers with their new responsibilities by expanding a pioneering program known as the Nurse-Family Partnership that offers home visits by trained registered nurses to low-income mothers and mothers-to-be.

This program has been proven to reduce childhood injuries, unintended pregnancies, and the use of welfare and food stamps. It's increased father involvement, women's employment, and children's school readiness. It's produced more than $28,000 in net savings for every high-risk family enrolled in the program. It works, and I'll expand the program to 570,000 first-time mothers each year.

The third part of my plan for urban America is to help people find work and make that work pay.

I will invest $1 billion over five years in innovative transitional jobs programs that have been highly successful at placing the unemployed into temporary jobs and then training them for permanent ones. People in these programs get the chance to work in a community service-type job, earn a paycheck every week, and learn the skills they need for gainful employment. And by leaving with references and a resume, often times they find that employment.

Still, even for those workers who do find a permanent job, many times there's no way for them to advance their careers once they're in those jobs. That's why we'll also work with community organizations and businesses to create career pathways that provide workers with the additional skills and training they need to earn more money. And we'll make sure that public transportation is both available and affordable for low-income workers, because no one should be denied work in this country because they can't get there.

To make work pay, I will also triple the Earned Income Tax Credit for full-time workers making the minimum wage. This is one of the most successful anti-poverty programs in history and lifts nearly 5 million Americans out of poverty every year. I was able to expand this program when I was a state Senator in Illinois, and as President I'll do it again.

The fourth part of my plan will be to help bring businesses back to our inner-cities. A long time ago, this country created a World Bank that has helped spur economic development in some of the world's poorest regions. I think it's about time we had something like that right here in America. Less than one percent of the $250 billion in venture capital that's invested each year goes to minority businesses that are trying to breathe life into our cities. This has to change.

When I'm President, I'll make sure that every community has the access to the capital and resources it needs to create a stronger business climate by providing more loans to small businesses and setting up the financial institutions that can help get them started. I'll also create a national network of business incubators, which are local services that help first-time business owners design their business plans, find the best location, and receive expert advice on how to run their businesses whenever they need it. And I will take steps to help close the digital divide and increase internet access for cities so that urban America is just as connected as the rest of America.

The final part of my plan to change the odds in our cities will be to ensure that more Americans have access to safe, affordable housing. As President, I'll create an Affordable Housing Trust Fund that would add as many as 112,000 new affordable units in mixed-income neighborhoods. We'll also do more to protect homeowners from mortgage fraud and subprime lending by passing my plan to provide counseling to tenants, homeowners, and other consumers so they get the advice and guidance they need before buying a house and support if they get into trouble down the road. And we will crack down on mortgage professionals found guilty of fraud by increasing enforcement and creating new criminal penalties.

Obligation to Keep Trying

What this agenda to combat urban poverty attempts to do is not easy, and it will not happen overnight. Changing the odds in our cities will require humility in what we can accomplish and patience with our progress. But most importantly, it will require the sustained commitment of the President of the United States, and that is why I will also appoint a new director of Urban Policy who will cut through the disorganized bureaucracy that currently exists and report directly to me on how these efforts are going; on what's working and what's not.

Because in the end, hope is found in what works.

The moral question about poverty in America—How can a country like this allow it?—has an easy answer: we can't. The political question that follows—What do we do about it?—has always been more difficult. But now that we're finally seeing the beginnings of an answer, this country has an obligation to keep trying.

The idea for the Harlem Children's Zone began with a list. It was a waiting list that Geoffrey Canada kept of all the children who couldn't get into his program back when it was just a few blocks wide. It was 500 people long. And one day he looked at that list and thought, why shouldn't those 500 kids get the same chance in life as the 500 who were already in the program? Why not expand it to include those 500? Why not 5000? Why not?

And that, of course, is the final question about poverty in America. It's the hopeful one that Bobby Kennedy was also famous for asking. Why not? It leaves the cynics without an answer, and it calls on the rest of us to get to work.

> "The feds spent billions . . . that did nothing to alleviate poverty."

Government Efforts to End Urban Poverty Are Counterproductive

Steven Malanga

In the following viewpoint, Steven Malanga opposes increased federal spending and interventions in fighting urban poverty. Citing efforts from past administrations, Malanga alleges that such policies turned welfare from temporary assistance into long-term handouts and did not develop communities, create more jobs, or serve the poor. Furthermore, federal aid did not raise student performance levels in public schools or provide affordable housing, he contends. Instead, Malanga maintains, cities succeeded when mayors fought crime, limited welfare, and provided vouchers for private schools. The author is a senior fellow at the Manhattan Institute and senior editor of its magazine, City Journal.

As you read, consider the following questions:

1. As explained by Malanga, what is "tin-cup urbanism"?

Steven Malanga, "We Don't Need Another War on Poverty," *City Journal*, vol. 18, August 2008. Reproduced by permission.

2. What theory did legislators of the war on poverty embrace, according to the author?

3. How did the mayors of New York and Milwaukee reduce welfare dependency, as stated by Malanga?

Do our cities need another War on Poverty? [then–presidential candidate] Barack Obama thinks so. Speaking before the U.S. Conference of Mayors this June [2008], the Democratic standard-bearer promised to boost spending on public schools, urban infrastructure, affordable housing, crime prevention, job training, and community organizing. The mayors, joined by many newspaper editorial pages, have echoed Obama in calling for vast new federal spending on cities. All of this has helped rejuvenate the old argument that America's urban areas are victims of Washington's neglect and that it's up to the rest of the country (even though most Americans are now metro-dwellers) to bail them out.

Nothing could be more misguided than to renew this "tincup urbanism," as some have called it. Starting in the late 1960s, mayors in struggling cities extended their palms for hundreds of billions of federal dollars that accomplished little good and often worsened the problems that they sought to fix. Beginning in the early nineties, however, a small group of reform-minded mayors—with New York's Rudy Giuliani and Milwaukee's John Norquist in the vanguard—jettisoned tincup urbanism and began developing their own bottom-up solutions to city problems. Their innovations made cities safer, put welfare recipients to work, and offered kids in failing school systems new choices, bringing about an incomplete, but very real, urban revival.

Yet this reform movement remains anathema [taboo] to many liberal politicians, academics, and journalists, who have ignored or tried to downplay its achievements because it conflicts with their left-of-center views. The arrival on the scene of Obama, a former Chicago community activist and the first presidential nominee in recent memory to rise out of urban politics, has given these back-to-the-future voices their best chance in years to advance a liberal War on Poverty-style agenda. As the nation debates its future in the current presidential race, it's crucial to remember what has worked to revive cities—and what hasn't.

The Original War on Poverty

The original War on Poverty, launched by the [Lyndon B.] Johnson administration in the mid-sixties, was based on the assumption that Washington had to rescue American cities from precipitous—indeed, catastrophic—decline. It's important to remember that the cities themselves helped propel that decline. Political machines had long run the cities, and they imposed increasingly high taxes and throttling regulations on employers and often entrusted key government agencies, including police departments, to patronage appointees. The cities' industrial might protected them from serious downturns for a time. But as transportation advances beginning in the 1950s enabled businesses to relocate to less expensive suburbs or newer Sunbelt cities, and did so just as a generation of poor, uneducated blacks from the rural South began migrating to the urban North, the corrupt and inefficient machines proved unable to cope with the resulting economic and demographic shock. Urban poverty worsened (even as poverty was shrinking dramatically elsewhere); crime exploded; public schools, dominated by reform-resistant, inflexible teachers' unions, became incubators of failure, with staggering dropout rates for minority students; and middle-class city dwellers soon followed businesses out of town. Some industrial cities, scarred further by horrific race riots during the sixties, crumbled into near-ruins.

Yet the War on Poverty's legislative architects ignored the cities' own failings and instead embraced the theories of left-wing intellectuals, who argued that the external forces arrayed against the poor, such as racism or globalization, were simply too overwhelming to address on the local level. "Officials and residents in urban communities are losing control of their cities to outside forces," warned urban planners Edward Kaitz and Herbert Harvey Hyman in their book *Urban Planning for Social Welfare.* "Cities are relatively powerless." The answer was federal intervention. Columbia University's Frances Fox Piven and Richard Cloward gained an influential following among policymakers by arguing that an unjust and racist nation owed massive government aid to the poor and mostly minority residents of struggling cities. Further, to compel those residents to work in exchange for help, or even to make them attend programs that might boost self-reliance, was to violate their civil liberties.

The War on Poverty, motivated by such toxic ideas, transformed welfare from temporary assistance into a lifelong stipend with few strings attached. As everyone knows, welfare rolls then skyrocketed, increasing 125 percent from 1965 to 1970 alone, and an entrenched generational underclass of poor families emerged. Typically, they lived in dysfunctional public housing projects—many of them built as another battle in the War—that radiated blight to surrounding neighborhoods. The federal government created a series of huge initiatives, from Medicaid and Head Start to food stamps and school lunch programs, that spent billions of dollars trying to fight urban poverty. And then, to attack the "root causes" of poverty (whatever they were), the feds spent billions more on local social-services agencies, which ran ill-defined programs with vague goals like "community empowerment" that did nothing to alleviate poverty.

Despite years of effort and gargantuan transfusions of money, the federal government lost its War on Poverty. "In 1968 . . . 13 percent of Americans were poor," wrote Charles Murray in his unstinting examination of antipoverty programs, *Losing Ground.* "Over the next 12 years, our expenditures on social welfare quadrupled. And in 1980, the percentage of poor Americans was—13 percent."

These programs did, however, produce a seismic shift in the way mayors viewed their cities—no longer as sources of dynamism and growth, as they had been for much of the nation's history, but instead as permanent, sickly wards of the federal government. In fact, as the problems of cities like Cleveland and New York festered and metastasized, mayors blamed the sickness on the federal government's failure to do even more. Norquist recalled a U.S. Conference of Mayors session held in the aftermath of the 1992 Los Angeles riots. "There was almost a feeling of glee among some mayors who attended: finally the federal government would realize it had to do something for cities."

A Different Approach

Even as tin-cup urbanism prevailed, however, some mayors began arguing for a different approach, based on the belief that cities could master their own futures. The nineties became an era of fruitful urban-policy experimentation. For instance, well before the federal welfare reform of 1996, various cities and counties, most notably Giuliani's New York and Norquist's Milwaukee (encouraged strongly by Wisconsin governor Tommy Thompson), not only set limits on welfare eligibility for the programs that they administered for the feds but also pursued a "work-first" policy that got able-bodied welfare recipients back into the workplace as swiftly as possible. Welfare rolls plummeted—in New York City, from 1.1 million in the early nineties to about 465,000 by 2001—and childhood poverty numbers decreased.

State and local legislators, often prodded by inner-city parents, also sought new ways to provide urban minority kids with a decent education. In Milwaukee, a former welfare mother, enraged that her children had no option other than the terrible public schools, helped push a school-voucher bill through the Wisconsin state legislature, letting disadvantaged students use public money to attend private schools. Most states passed laws enabling private groups to set up charter schools unencumbered by many of the union-backed rules found in public school systems, such as restrictions on firing lousy teachers. Today, some 4,300 charter schools, many in big cities, educate 1.2 million kids nationally—and most are performing, studies show, better than nearby public schools.

The era's most impressive urban reform improved public safety. Under Giuliani and his first police commissioner, William Bratton, New York City famously embraced Broken Windows policing, in which cops enforced long-dormant laws against public disorder, fostering a new climate of respect for the right of all citizens to use public spaces. The nineties' NYPD [New York Police Department] also introduced computer technology that tracked and mapped shifting crime patterns, so that police could respond quickly whenever and wherever crime spiked upward, and new accountability measures to ensure that commanders followed through. Crime in New York has plummeted 70 percent since the implementation of these reforms—double the national decline. Other cities that have adopted similar policing methods, from Newark to East Orange, New Jersey, to Raleigh, North Carolina, have had big crime turnarounds, too. As Newark mayor Cory Booker, who tapped an NYPD veteran as police director, noted about crime-fighting: "There are models in America, right in New York City, that show that this is not an issue of *can* we, but *will* we."

Ignoring the Lessons

Obama may claim to be advancing a twenty-first-century agenda, but his ideas about combating poverty and aiding cities ignore the lessons of the nineties' reformers and remain firmly mired in the War on Poverty's vision of cities as victims. Nothing betrays his urban agenda's retrograde nature more than its Number One spending item: a big hike in funding for the Community Development Block Grant [CDBG] program. The candidate calls this relic of the War on Poverty "an important program that provides housing and creating [*sic*] jobs for low- and moderate-income people and places." In fact, the block grants are perhaps the most visible example of the failure of federal urban aid, plagued, as so much other War on Poverty spending was plagued, by vague goals, a failure to demand concrete results from the groups it funds, and a reputation for political patronage. CDBG money, amounting to some $110 billion over its history, has financed many projects that have zilch to do with fighting poverty—an opera house, a zoo, tennis courts, and historical restorations, for instance. A stark example of the program's failure to achieve its ostensible mission: Buffalo, [New York,] the city that has received the most community redevelopment funding per capita, is economically worse off today than it was 40 years ago.

Nevertheless, CDBG spending is often invoked as evidence that the federal government is "doing something" about urban problems. This was the case in 1993, when the [Bill] Clinton administration authorized a massive $430 million block grant to establish a loan fund to help Los Angeles recover from the previous year's devastating riots, as well as millions more to ameliorate "the underlying causes of the unrest." Within two years, though, a third of the companies that the loan money had financed had gone belly-up or fallen behind in payments, while two-thirds hadn't fulfilled their obligations to create new jobs in the city. As for the money aimed at "underlying causes," local officials merely spent it on yet more ineffective community groups.

Obama doubtless will claim that he can fix this kind of urban aid to make it more accountable, but the obstacles are great. The [George W.] Bush administration, for instance, sought to junk most of the program and focus what remained on narrow projects with specific, measurable antipoverty goals.

But congressional CDBG backers on both sides of the aisle, who insert millions of dollars in earmarks into it each year, derailed the reform.

Backward Solutions

Though Obama has supported some education reforms, such as charter schools, his plan for fixing urban schools by showering more federal money on them is another attempt to revive tin-cup largesse. In his signature education speech, Obama described visiting a high school outside Chicago that "couldn't afford to keep teachers for a full day, so school let out at 1:30 every afternoon," adding that "stories like this can be found across America." Later, he said: "We cannot ask our teachers to perform the impossible, to teach poorly prepared children with inadequate resources."

In fact, the U.S. has made vast investments in its public schools. According to a study by Manhattan Institute scholar Jay Greene, per-student spending on K–12 public education in the U.S. rocketed from $2,345 in the mid-1950s to $8,745 in 2002 (both figures in 2009 dollars). Per-pupil spending in many cities is lavish. In New York, huge funding increases dating to the late 1990s have pushed per-pupil spending to $19,000; across the river in Newark, state and federal aid has boosted per-pupil expenditures to above $20,000; and Washington, D.C., now spends more than $22,000 a year per student. Yet these urban school systems have shown little or no improvement. "Schools are not inadequately funded—they would not perform substantially better if they had more money," Greene observes. An Organisation for Economic Cooperation and Development study found that most European countries spend between 55 percent and 70 percent of what the U.S. does per student, yet produce better educational outcomes. If some urban school systems are failing children, money has nothing to do with it.

Obama also promises to invest heavily in the human capital of cities, seeking to forge a smarter, better-trained urban workforce. Yet here, too, his solutions look backward. His key proposal to help the chronically unemployable find work is simply to reauthorize the Workforce Investment Act [WIA] of 1998. But politically connected insiders run many of the WIA's job-training initiatives, and waste is widespread. One Government Accountability Office [GAO] study found that only about 40 percent of the $2.4 billion that the WIA designates for retraining dislocated workers actually went to the workers themselves; administrative costs gobbled up the rest. Even the money that reaches workers does little obvious good. In congressional testimony [in 2007], a GAO official said, "We have little information at a national level about what the workforce investment system under WIA achieves."

Another big-ticket, War on Poverty-style item on Obama's agenda is to give cities more federal money to build "affordable" housing. Yet even as mayors warn about a critical shortage of housing for the poor and the middle class, many simultaneously claim that they are hemorrhaging population because of competition from suburbs—and that should be lowering housing costs. Further, with foreclosures rising rapidly in some cities, cheap housing should be plentiful.

What explains this conundrum are the local policies that have helped make housing unaffordable. In a study called "The Planning Penalty," economist Randal O'Toole points out that half a century ago, when many cities were still gaining population, almost all of them boasted a healthy stock of affordable housing. Yet starting in the 1970s, cities began aggressively limiting and directing housing growth, enacting rules for minimum lot sizes and population density that produced significant cost increases for builders, who passed them on to consumers. In Trenton, New Jersey, O'Toole estimates that the city-imposed planning penalty adds $49,000, or 17 percent, to the median cost of a home in a city where the population has shrunk from 130,000 in the 1950s to 85,000 today. In nearby Newark, a city pockmarked with empty lots that has lost some 170,000 residents, the planning penalty is $154,000, adding 41 percent to median home value. In New York, where Mayor Michael Bloomberg has committed $7.5 billion to build 165,000 units of affordable housing over ten years, the additional costs heaped on by government planning reach a whopping $311,000 per home. There's zero evidence that Obama understands the planning penalty at the heart of the affordable-housing shortage in many cities.

Obama and the U.S. Conference of Mayors also call for an increase in HOPE VI funding as a way of getting welfare families to stop thinking of public housing as a permanent entitlement. The HOPE VI program, launched in the early nineties, got cities to replace large projects with smaller communities where the subsidized poor would live among those who could afford market-rate housing. The hope was that the bourgeois values of those earning their way in life would somehow rub off on the recipients of housing subsidies, and that they would then move up and out. But because the program imposed no actual requirements on the poor, the effort failed. Research has shown that in cities like Memphis, where the poor have been dispersed to middle-class neighborhoods, crime is rising.

Judging by these and other Obama initiatives, an urban-reform agenda based on the bottom-up successes of the 1990s still awaits its national advocate. It would start from the notion that cities can indeed be masters of their own futures. It would encourage city self-empowerment, not victimhood. Above all, it would urge municipalities to build on the stunning urban-policy successes of the 1990s. . . .

Obama's rise has put urban issues back into the presidential campaign for the first time in decades. But so far, the discussion that his candidacy has sparked is taking place largely among politicians, commentators, and interest groups whose view of cities hasn't moved on much from the War on Poverty. Implementing their policy ideas would simply expand the tin-cup urbanism that has kept so many cities in despair for so long. That's change we can do without.

"*A disorderly environment sends a message that no one is in charge, thus . . . inviting criminal behavior.*"

Urban Blight Contributes to Crime

Carolyn Y. Johnson

In the following viewpoint, Carolyn Y. Johnson supports the "broken windows" theory, in which urban blight creates the impression that police or community control is absent, inviting criminal activity. The author writes that a recent Boston study demonstrated the clean up and maintenance of crime-ridden hot spots resulted in 20 percent fewer calls to police, more effective than misdemeanor arrests and increasing social services. The theory is debated, but additional research reinforces the premise that more criminal behavior occurs in disorderly environments, she says. Johnson is a Boston Globe *staff writer.*

As you read, consider the following questions:

1. According to the author, how were crime hot spots cleaned up?

2. What occurred in the Netherlands study, according to Johnson?

Carolyn Y. Johnson, "Breakthrough on 'Broken Windows,'" *Boston Globe*, February 8, 2009. Reprinted by permission.

3. What does Chen-Bo Zhong, as cited by the author, assert about environmental influences on behavior and thinking?

The year was 2005 and Lowell [Massachusetts] was being turned into a real life crime-fighting laboratory.

Researchers, working with police, identified 34 crime hot spots. In half of them, authorities set to work—clearing trash from the sidewalks, fixing street lights, and sending loiterers scurrying. Abandoned buildings were secured, businesses forced to meet code, and more arrests made for misdemeanors. Mental health services and homeless aid referrals expanded.

In the remaining hot spots, normal policing and services continued.

Then researchers from Harvard and Suffolk University sat back and watched, meticulously recording criminal incidents in each of the hot spots.

The results, just now circulating in law enforcement circles, are striking: A 20 percent plunge in calls to police from the parts of town that received extra attention. It is seen as strong scientific evidence that the long-debated "broken windows" theory really works—that disorderly conditions breed bad behavior, and that fixing them can help prevent crime.

"In traditional policing, you went from call to call, and that was it—you're chasing your tail," said Lowell patrol officer Karen Witts on a recent drive past a boarded up house that was once a bullet-pocked trouble spot. Now, she says, there appears to be a solid basis for a policing strategy that preemptively addresses the conditions that promote crime.

Many police departments across the country already use elements of the broken windows theory, or focus on crime hot spots. The Lowell experiment offers guidance on what seems to work best. Cleaning up the physical environment was very effective; misdemeanor arrests less so, and boosting social services had no apparent impact.

Such evidence-based policing is essential, argues David Weisburd, a professor of administration of justice at George Mason University. "We demand it in fields like medicine," Weisburd said. "It seems to me with all the money we spend on policing, we better be able to see whether the programs have the effects we intend them to have."

And this particular study, he said, is "elegant" in how clearly it demonstrated crime prevention benefits.

The broken windows theory was first put forth in a 1982 *Atlantic* article by James Q. Wilson, a political scientist then at Harvard, and George L. Kelling, a criminologist. The theory suggests that a disorderly environment sends a message that no one is in charge, thus increasing fear, weakening community controls, and inviting criminal behavior. It further maintains that stopping minor offenses and restoring greater order can prevent serious crime.

That theory has been hotly debated even as it has been widely deployed.

Critics have pointed out that defining "disorder" is inherently subjective. Some challenge "broken windows" success stories, questioning, for example, whether New York City's decrease in crime in the 1990s could have been caused by the decline in the use of crack cocaine or other factors.

Bernard Harcourt, a professor of law and political science at the University of Chicago who has been critical of the broken windows policing method, called the Lowell experiment fascinating because it showed that changing the nature of a place had a stronger effect on crime than misdemeanor arrests.

"It helps practitioners," said Brenda J. Bond, assistant professor of public management at Suffolk. "We need to . . . focus on hot-spot areas like this using these kinds of tools and techniques." With lead author Anthony Braga, a senior research associate at Harvard Kennedy School, Bond co-wrote the study detailing the findings, published in August [2008] in the journal *Criminology*.

The work has directly influenced policing in Boston, said police commissioner Edward Davis, who was chief in Lowell during the study. In Boston, Davis has created "safe street teams" that target disorder in 10 crime hot spots.

"We've given them a special number at City Hall to call for removal of graffiti, any kind of disorder, any broken windows, any trash in the street," Davis said. "You have to prove to the officers it works, and doing this type of experimentation, having findings published, goes a long way."

The strategies continue to flourish across Lowell. "Sometimes, we create mini-task forces to saturate an area at a particular time of day when we see disorder," Lowell police Superintendent Kenneth Lavallee said. "We target those activities that could be a quality of life issue, like drinking, motor vehicle enforcement."

As Witts, the patrol officer, drove around the city last week, she pointed out evidence of success. A brick apartment building that once racked up 100 calls to police in a three-month period has, she said, had just one incident over the last six weeks. Gone, she noted, are the unregistered cars in the parking lot, the broken fence, and the code violations in the building—as well as problem tenants and crime.

The Lowell study is not the only support being given to the broken windows theory. A second study, published in the journal *Science* in December, reported on how it held up in individual experiments in Europe.

In one, researchers staked out an alley in Groningen, Netherlands, where people parked their bikes. They attached fliers to handlebars in one setting that was clean, and one in which the walls were covered with graffiti. They found that only a third of the participants tossed the fliers on the pavement in the clean alley, whereas more than two-thirds did so in the less orderly environment.

Untended Property Invites Crime

Untended property becomes fair game for people out for fun or plunder, and even for people who ordinarily would not dream of doing such things and who probably consider themselves law-abiding. Because of the nature of community life in the Bronx [New York City]—its anonymity, the frequency with which cars are abandoned and things are stolen or broken, the past experience of "no one caring"—vandalism begins much more quickly than it does in staid Palo Alto, where people have come to believe that private possessions are cared for and that mischievous behavior is costly. But vandalism can occur anywhere once communal barriers—the sense of mutual regard and the obligations of civility—are lowered by actions that seem to signal that "no one cares."

James Q. Wilson and George L. Kelling,
Atlantic, March 1982.

In a second experiment, researchers tried to stimulate a crime. Letters that clearly contained money were left sticking out of mailboxes, one in a clean neighborhood, and one in a neighborhood where the mailbox was covered with graffiti.

In the clean neighborhood, 13 percent of passersby stole the envelope, while in the disorderly neighborhood, 27 percent did.

Beyond broken windows theory, psychologists are studying how the environment influences behavior and thinking.

"One of the implications certainly is that efforts that invest in improving the environment in terms of cleanliness may actually help in reducing moral transgressions because people perceive higher moral standards," said Chen-Bo Zhong, assistant professor of management at the Rotman School of Management at the University of Toronto.

All of which plays out in the theory that Wilson and Kelling introduced in 1982.

"Think of how long it took," Kelling, a Rutgers professor said of the latest evidence. "If you're a police executive or a policy executive, you can't wait 27 years—you have to make good policy decisions based on bad data and good theory and correlation."

| *"There is no good evidence for the theory that disorder causes crime."*

Urban Blight Does Not Contribute to Crime

C.R. Sridhar

C.R. Sridhar is a lawyer in Bangalore, India. In the following viewpoint, Sridhar contests the theory of "broken windows," which posits that urban blight and signs of minor disobedience encourage more serious offenses. Proponents argue the theory was successfully applied by the New York Police Department in the 1990s, but the author states that other factors contributed to the city's significant drop in crime, such as the booming economy, transformation of the drug trade, population changes, and the statistical ebb and flow of criminal activity. Sridhar further states that the broken windows theory is problematic because it targets minorities and the poor for police harassment.

As you read, consider the following questions:

1. As described by Sridhar, what happened to individuals loitering on the streets of New York City under zero tolerance?

C.R. Sridhar, "Policing Urban Crimes: The Broken Windows Theory," BlogCritics, September 26, 2006. Reproduced by permission.

2. What evidence does Bernard E. Harcourt, as cited by the author, provide to counter the broken windows theory?

3. In Sridhar's view, how did the "learning effect" reduce crime in New York City?

"He who steals an egg steals an ox."—A French saying quoted from *The 'Scholarly Myths' of the New Law and Order Doxa* by Loïc Wacquant.

Just two days before the French riots of Oct 27, 2005, sparked by the deaths of two African teenagers in the underprivileged northeastern suburbs of Paris, the [then] French Interior Minister Nicolas Sarkozy famously remarked, *"Vous en avez assez de cette bande de racaille? Eh bien, on va vous en débarrasser."* ("You've had enough of the dregs of society? Well, we're going to get rid of them for you.") The Interior Minister took a tough stand on fighting crime on the streets by saying that certain cities in France needed "nettoyer au Kärcher" (power washing).

These comments proved inflammatory among the poor African youth, already facing racism, and the riots soon spread to nearly 300 cities of France leading to widespread torching of cars and destruction of public property.

From the perspective of criminology, Mr. Sarkozy's semantics about fighting crime and enforcing order is certainly colourful and controversial but conceptually not a novel idea. His police strategy towards urban crime is borrowed from the key concepts of broken windows and zero tolerance enunciated in American criminology. In fact, "over the past several years French politicians (as well as their English, Italian, Spanish, and German colleagues) of the Left as well as the Right," writes Loïc Wacquant, "have travelled as one on a pilgrimage, to signify their newfound resolve to crush the scourge of street crime and, for this purpose, to initiate themselves into the concepts and measures adopted by the U.S. authorities." This new security doxa [an unquestioned opinion] found favour with liberals as it was perceived as a rational policy resting on effectiveness and seemingly devoid of any ideological bias.

The concept of broken windows was developed by James Q. Wilson and George L. Kelling who published their article titled *Broken Windows: The Police and Neighborhood Safety* in the March 1982 edition of *The Atlantic Monthly*. The authors posited their theory in the following words "Social psychologists and police officers tend to agree that if a window in a building is broken and is left unrepaired, all the rest of the windows will soon be broken. This is as true in nice neighborhoods as in run-down ones. Window breaking does not necessarily occur on a large scale because some areas are inhabited by determined window-breakers whereas others are populated by window-lovers; rather, one unrepaired broken window is a signal that no one cares, and so breaking more windows costs nothing (it has always been fun)." "The essence of broken windows," explains Charles Pollard, "is that minor incivilities (such as drunkenness, begging, vandalism, disorderly behaviour, graffiti, litter etc.), if unchecked and uncontrolled, produce an atmosphere in a community or on a street in which more serious crime will flourish." In other words, crimes flourish because of lax enforcement.

The prescription for broken windows is to shift policing from major crimes to traditional public order maintenance. As Wilson and Kelling note, "A great deal was accomplished during this transition, as both police chiefs and outside experts emphasized the crime-fighting function in their plans, in the allocation of resources, and in deployment of personnel. The police may well have become better crime-fighters as a result. And doubtless they remained aware of their responsibility for order. But the link between order-maintenance and crime-prevention, so obvious to earlier generations, was forgotten."

Putting Theory into Practice

Nearly a decade after the publication of the article, the theory of broken windows was put into practice by the Republican Mayor Rudy Guiliani across New York City. He appointed William Bratton as the Commissioner of the New York Police Department (NYPD) in 1994. The Guiliani-Bratton team honed to perfection a police strategy called zero tolerance, which some scholars point out was derived from the broken windows theory to tackle the high incidence of crimes in New York City. Bratton explains the theory in his paper *Crime Is Down in New York City: Blame the Police.*

The paper lucidly expounds the specific strategy used in fighting street disorder and crimes, which plagued the streets of New York. A close reading of the paper gives one the impression that there was heavy emphasis on concentrated aggression and ruthless prosecution of petty crimes. Bratton chose to focus police action on subway fare evaders and homeless people who lived in the subways of New York. Soon the subways were declared crime free and reclaimed for the benefit of the citizens. Other offenders targeted were jaywalkers, the squeegee men (individuals who cleaned the windshields of cars trapped in traffic snarls and coercing the motorists to pay for their services), panhandlers, drunks, noisy teenagers and streetwalkers [prostitutes].

The aggressive policing included searches, sweeps and arrests of individuals found loitering in streets even though they had not committed any crime under law. There was reorganization of the police force by flattening hierarchies and empowering the captains of precincts. Police officers were judged by statistical figures of arrests they made and promotions given. The police forces were expanded significantly from 27,000 (1993) to 41,000 (2001). Information technology was deployed and officers had greater access to computers. There was compilation of crime statistics, sharing of data, which made police deployments to crime-affected areas more effective. Under Bratton, the NYPD became a formidable machine with an offensive outlook on crime and disorder.

There is general agreement among academicians of criminal jurisprudence that crime in New York did drop. Murder decreased by 72% and total violent crimes by 51%.

The remarkable turnaround in crime rates were largely seen as attributable to broken windows or its semantic variant, quality-of-life policing adopted by NYPD. Conservative policy makers lauded the efforts of Giuliani and Bratton in cleaning the streets of New York and assertively claimed that other states would do well to follow the Bratton Miracle. The influential Manhattan Institute together with the Giuliani Group has been propagating the policing philosophy to Latin America for curbing urban crimes. In the year 1998 alone . . . police officials from 150 countries visited NYPD to learn about the innovative techniques of crime control.

The Eye of a Perfect Storm

In recent years the broken windows theory and the order maintenance strategy has been in the eye of a perfect storm. A note of dissent was struck by Bernard E. Harcourt, a Visiting Professor of Law at Harvard University, who said, "the difficulty is that there is no good evidence for the theory that disorder causes crime. To the contrary, the most reliable social scientific evidence suggests that the theory is wrong. The popularity of the broken windows theory, it turns out, is inversely related to the quality of the supporting evidence."

Harcourt backs his conclusion by relying on a comprehensive study conducted by Robert Sampson and Stephen Raudenbush on disorder in urban neighbourhoods. This study was based on careful data collection using trained observers. On a random basis, 15,141 streets of Chicago were selected for analysis. Sampson and Raudenbush found that disorder and predatory crime are moderately correlated, but that, when antecedent neighbourhood characteristics (such as neighbourhood trust and poverty) are taken into account, the connection between disorder and crime "vanished in 4 out of 5 tests—including homicide, arguably our best measure of violence." Sampson and Raudenbush conclude that attacking public order through tough police tactics may thus be a politically popular but perhaps analytically weak strategy to reduce crime.

Similar doubts were voiced by other research scholars who expressed grave reservation about adopting the New York style of policing. On the basis of a cross-city comparison of policing strategies and homicide rates, Anna Joanes observed that all of this attention has not been positive, as many NYC residents and observers have blamed this policy for the rise in police brutality and racial tensions and the loss of trust and respect for the police. New York has not achieved a greater crime reduction than that of all other U.S. cities. In fact, the three cyclical measures reveal that New York City's decline was either equal to or below that of several other large cities, including San Francisco, San Jose, Cleveland, San Diego, Washington, St. Louis and Houston. These other cities employ a variety of policing strategies. The fact that cities like San Diego and San Francisco employed different policing strategies but have experienced similar declines in their crime rates calls into question the claim that the NYPD's tactics have produced an unrivaled decrease in crime.

According to Wacquant it is not the police who make crime go away. A trenchant critic of Giuliani-Bratton police work, Waquant puts forth the view that six factors independent of police work have significantly reduced crime rates in America. First, the *boom in economy* provided jobs for youth and diverted them from street crimes. Even though the official poverty rate of New York City remained unchanged at 20% during the entire decade of the 1990s, Latinos benefited by the deskilled labour market. The blacks, buoyed by the hope of the flourishing economy, went back to school and avoided illegal trade. Thus even though under-employment and low paid work persisted there was decline of aggregate unemployment rates which explains 30% decrease in national crime rates.

Second, *there was twofold transformation in drug trade.* The retail trade in crack in poor neighbourhoods attained stability. The turf wars subsided and violent competition among rival gangs decreased. The narcotic sector had become oligopolised [dominated by a small number of sellers]. This resulted in a sharp drop in drug related street murders. In 1998 it dropped below the 100 mark from 670 murders in 1991. The change in consumption of drugs went from crack to other drugs such as marijuana, heroin and methamphetamines, a trade which is less violent as it is based on networks of mutual acquaintances rather than anonymous exchange places.

Third, the *number of young people (age group between 18– 24) declined.* It must be noted that the young people in this age group are found most responsible for crimes. The AIDS epidemic among drug users, drug overdose deaths, gang related homicides and young criminals imprisoned decreased this group by 43,000. This decline of young people resulted in the drop of street crimes by one-tenth.

Fourth, the impact of *learning effect* that the deaths of earlier generations of young people had on the later generation, especially those born after 1975–1980, avoided drugs and stayed away from risky lifestyles.

Fifth, the role played by churches, schools, clubs and other organizations in *awareness and prevention campaigns* exercised informal social control and helped to control crimes.

Sixth, the *statistical law of regression* states that when there is abnormally high incidence of crime it is likely to decline and settle towards the mean. Wacquant concludes that the dynamic interplay of the six factors was largely responsible for

The Validity of the "Broken Windows" Theory Is Unknown

The validity of the broken windows theory is not known. It is safe to conclude that the theory does not explain everything and that, even if the theory is valid, companion theories are necessary to fully explain crime. Alternatively, a more complex model is needed to consider many more cogent factors. Almost every study of the topic has, however, validated the link between disorder and fear. There is also strong support for the belief that fear increases a person's desire to abandon disorderly communities and move to environments that are more hospitable.

Adam J. McKee, David Levinson, ed.,
Encyclopedia of Crime and Punishment, Volume I, *2002.*

the drop in crime rates in America and the claim that policing alone was responsible for the drop in crimes at best rests on shaky empirical data.

A Slippery Theoretical Slope

The concept of broken windows rests on a slippery theoretical slope. More problematic is the underlying notion that focusing "police activity on those social categories presumed to be crime vectors" could prevent crimes. The danger inherent in such a notion is that the police functionaries would be in a position to extra-legally harass the homeless, the destitute and the minorities. This has been well documented by law enforcement officials, academics and human rights groups. In a study conducted in 1999 by the [former] New York Attorney General Eliot Spitzer with the help of Columbia University's Centre for Violence Research and Prevention, Spitzer concluded "in aggregate across all crime categories and precincts citywide, blacks were 'stopped' 23% more often (in comparison to the crime rate) than whites. Hispanics were 'stopped' 39% more often than whites." The racially discriminatory pattern is evident from the statistics available for the U.S. as a whole and for New York City, which shows that adults arrested for misdemeanors are disproportionately African American in relation to their representation in the community.

The experience in other parts of the world has not been an encouraging one. For instance, The New South Wales Council for Civil Liberties has recorded that the zero tolerance policing has been racially discriminatory to the Arabic-speaking people. Similarly, in South Africa there have been doubts whether zero tolerance would be acceptable to the public, as the memories of the repressive apartheid regime remains fresh in the minds of the people.

In the final analysis, the implementation of order maintenance policing may destroy the diversity and vitality of democratic society. As Bernard Harcourt eloquently sums up:

"It is, in effect, a type of 'aesthetic policing' that fosters a sterile, Disneyland, consumerist, commercial aesthetic. It reflects a desire to transform New York City into Singapore, or worse, a shopping mall. The truth is, however, that when we lose the dirt, grit, and street life of major American cities, we may also threaten their vitality, creativity, and character."

> "In the United States 49 percent of the urban homeless are African American (compared to 11 percent of the general population)."

Urban Homelessness Is a Serious Problem for African Americans

Maco L. Faniel

African Americans are the face of urban homelessness contends Maco L. Faniel in the following viewpoint. The minority group makes up almost half of the people living on city streets across the nation, he claims, even though African Americans compose only 11 percent of the general population. Faniel insists that the government and citizens ignore urban homelessness because of racism and the misperception that homelessness is a choice, not the result of a lack of affordable housing, generational poverty, mental or substance abuse issues, and other social problems. The author is a contributing writer to Regal Magazine, *a publication for African American men.*

As you read, consider the following questions:

1. How does Faniel characterize the problem of homelessness in the United States?

2. In the author's view, why are the homeless unemployed?

3. How did Noah Ratler experience homelessness as an African American, according to Faniel?

You see them every time that you drive downtown to go to work or take care of some important business. You see them sleeping under bridges or at intersections with signs that read "WILL WORK FOR FOOD!" You see them on the local news station in line getting food during the holidays. And you see them sleeping on the ground when you are standing in line for Black Friday [the Friday following Thanksgiving when holiday shopping begins]! Who are THEY? They are the nameless faces of urban homelessness. They are the 3.5 million men, women, and children who live on the streets in the richest nation in the world.

And though they are nameless, and for most of us unknown, their face is almost the same city to city across this nation. IT'S A BLACK FACE OF URBAN HOMELESSNESS. Yes, in the United States 49 percent of the urban homeless are African American (compared to 11 percent of the general population) and in Houston 66.7 percent of the urban homeless are African American men (compared to 25 percent of Houston's general population).

Urban homelessness is America's shameful secret that we try to hide in the corners of our metropolitan areas as if the problem does not exist.

Could it be that urban homelessness is neglected by most of America because the faces of those who are homeless are overwhelmingly BLACK?

Making the Homeless Invisible

Whether urban homelessness is a race issue or not, we all contribute in some way to the problem. The individual nature of our society and economy has conditioned us to ignore urban homelessness, thus we make the victims of urban homelessness invisible. Yes, it is easy to say "GO GET A JOB, YOU LAZY BUM," but consider this for a moment: you are a homeless Black man in America who sleeps under the freeway; you wake up every morning in search of food and employment. But here is the kicker—when you go look for a job you have to take all of your stuff with you because all of your life possessions fit into one bag. Employers are afraid to hire you because you are an un-groomed, stinky, Black man who carries a bag around—they know immediately that you are homeless. You can't get your hair cut, and you have to wear the same clothes every day. And though you really want to work and get on your feet, you feel discouraged because there is so much up against you.

It is difficult to "GO GET A JOB" when you are not well nourished. It is difficult to "GO GET A JOB" when you slept on the concrete the night before. It is difficult to "GO GET A JOB" when you have not had a bath or when your clothes stink. It is difficult to "GO GET A JOB" when your basic human rights have been stripped and when your dignity has been diminished. It is difficult to "GO GET A JOB" when you don't feel like a whole person.

Contrary to popular belief, people are not homeless because they don't want to work, however; there are several reasons that engender urban homelessness including: lack of affordable housing, generational poverty, substance abuse, mental health issues, unsupported release from incarceration, re-entry from military service, or domestic violence.

Getting Attention

Whatever the reason, the problem was so bad for Noah Ratler that he decided to do something about it. In 2007, Ratler took a journey by foot from Houston to Los Angles (the epicenter of the urban homeless epidemic) to bring attention to urban homelessness.

"At first I was just going to walk to the Grand Canyon as a personal goal. As I was planning the trip I figured out that personal goal could mean more to more people. And being that I was volunteering at a local homeless organization at the time and taking in what I was learning through my experience, it could be beneficial to talk about homelessness as I walked. Once it became about homelessness, Los Angeles was a logical conclusion, because it is only 500 miles further, and has the largest homeless population," says Ratler.

Ratler really wanted to find out how the "mentally ill are treated in our society." And when he began that journey, it led him immediately to urban homelessness. Ratler says that "I used to look at the homeless and pass them by not understanding their situation. Because there is an apathy that occupies the hearts of our society that allows us to look past them. If we were to look at them, we would see ourselves in their eyes. People don't care to find out what is going on, there is lack of caring, it is like forced objectivity. Our system is set up to promote the individual above the family, it promotes self-interest. In promoting self-interest, we focus inwardly, and those who are in our group are all who matter. Those who are outside become the enemy, even if that is by not acting to save someone outside our group, when we have the power to save their lives."

The Same Struggles

While on the road, Ratler got the opportunity to experience life as a transient Black homeless man—he was able to see how homeless people are treated—"It was different each of the 134 days on the road. When I was in Navaho country, I would see cats hanging out on the corner, drunks, dope heads, that looked just like a scene from my 'hood, but they were not Black. Everything looked the same, a different setting, with

Homelessness and African American Women

The number of homeless women is increasing in the United States, with African American women dispropor-tionately represented among this too vulnerable popula-tion. The number of homeless people approaching 50 years of age is expected to increase dramatically, and older African American women are particularly vulner-able to homelessness. Reasons associated with increased homelessness include unmet need for affordable housing and growing numbers of baby boomers reaching older adulthood, especially prior to qualifying for entitlements available to those classified as being legally old. The cur-rent [2009] economic crisis and the ripple effects of prob-lematic housing policies are likely to accelerate the num-ber of homeless people and include those taking refuge on the streets, in shelters, and in homes of friends and extended family.

Olivia Washington, Holly Feen-Calligan, and David Moxley,
Visual Culture & Gender, vol. 4, 2009.

different people, but their struggles were the same as people that I knew. I was looked at as if I was homeless. When I was on my way to Ft. Worth, I had not shaved or got a hair cut since I left Houston. I yelled across the street to ask a woman for directions, and she yelled back, 'I DON'T HAVE ANY MONEY!' That same day, I tried to go into a couple of rest-rooms, and they would not let me in, everybody would just look at me when I would try to get something to eat. That is when I started to piece it together; this is what it is like. People would stare at me. When people don't recognize the humanity in you, it is hard, a hard thing to live with," says Ratler.

Ratler's advocacy journey took him all the way to Skid Row in Los Angeles, but it did not stop there. He was so taken aback by the problem that he decided to begin the Houston SleepOut in 2008. He says that Houston SleepOut "is an event that allows people to make a contribution towards S.E.A.R.C.H. Homeless Services, an organization that serves over 10,000 homeless per year, in the city of Houston. The contribution is made by individuals raising money from their friends and family, and coming together with other individuals who have done the same thing to spend one night without a home. In doing that, they don't get to really understand what homelessness is, but my hope is that they get the little insight into how their situation can be different."

We Are Connected

When asked what you think a person can do to eradicate homelessness, Ratler said, "I would ask anybody to educate themselves on it. That is my main push, awareness to educate everybody about homelessness, at least [to] introduce it. There is no one answer, it's just something that you have to think about, and in thinking about it, something will come out. After you educate yourself, find out a piece of the problem that you can do to help it. That could include sending a check, it includes volunteering your time, or if you really get into it, you will find a creative way; your time, your talent, your tokens."

Dr. Martin Luther King, Jr. said that "an individual has not started living until he can rise above the narrow confines of his individualistic concerns to the broader concerns of all humanity." And in order to do this, we must all realize that we are connected—that our actions in say College Park, Atlanta, directly affect a child in Darfur [Sudan] or a homeless person in Houston. Noah Ratler, a kid from the South Park neighborhood in Houston, understands it like this, "I am connected to kids from Ikeja, [Nigeria;] Rio de Janeiro, [Brazil;] kids in India, kids in Palestine, kids in [the elite Houston neighborhood of] River Oaks. And we all create the world that we live in. We are connected physically, by genetic makeup. We are 99 percent the same; on a more existential level we are connected through the effects of all of our actions. For me to wear a neck tie here, there is a city in China [that] is designed to build neck ties. So if we all decide to stop wearing neck ties, then there is a city that dies."

Ratler did something, are you willing?

> "A new approach . . . has revolutionized urban programs and brought major reductions in the chronically homeless populations of U.S. cities."

New Programs Can Help End Urban Homelessness

Ian Merrifield

In the following viewpoint, Ian Merrifield claims that a new approach promises to end urban homelessness. He states that the "Ten-Year Plans to End Chronic Homelessness" effectively combine housing with treatment for addiction and mental illness, the two major underlying causes of homelessness. Additionally, the author argues that the plans are economically advantageous—the annual costs (including police monitoring, medical emergencies, etc.) of allowing a person to live on the street exceed the costs of providing housing and counseling for the same period of time. When this viewpoint was published in 2009, Merrifield was an undergraduate student majoring in government at Harvard University.

Ian Merrifield, "The Ten-Year Plan," *Harvard Political Review*, May 24, 2009. http://hpronline.org/urban-america/the-ten-year-plan/. Reprinted with permission.

As you read, consider the following questions:

1. What is Merrifield's position on shelters and soup kitchens?

2. How does the author support his assertion that most of the chronic homeless suffer from addiction or mental illness?

3. How does Philip Mangano, as cited by Merrifield, respond to arguments against the "Ten-Year Plans"?

While the recent collapse of the U.S. housing market has prompted a renewed debate about American homeownership and its future, the related topic of homelessness has remained largely ignored. Hundreds of thousands of citizens live lives of addiction and mental illness on the streets of American cities. On any given day, 900,000 people—including 200,000 children—go to sleep homeless in the United States, and the current economic crisis has only increased these numbers. Until very recently, the conventional approach toward combating homelessness did not focus on effectively solving the problem but rather on serving the homeless sporadically in soup kitchens and shelters. Although certainly valuable, this work had not caused any significant reductions in the numbers of the chronically homeless in major U.S. cities.

Yet a new approach by the U.S. Interagency Council on Homelessness, led by "Homelessness Czar" Philip Mangano, has revolutionized urban programs and brought major reductions in the chronically homeless populations of U.S. cities. Taking advantage of what Mangano, in an interview with the HPR [*Harvard Political Review*], called a new climate of "unprecedented political will and unprecedented resources" to "dare to put the verb 'end' with the noun 'homelessness,'" the Council has helped 350 American cities and counties implement "Ten-Year Plans to End Chronic Homelessness." These plans prioritize ending homelessness by providing housing and counseling for addiction and illness rather than serving the homeless from the streets. Though the plans have been criticized for focusing too intently on assisting those who are already homeless rather than helping those at risk of homelessness stay in their homes, their success at reducing the chronically homeless population is irrefutable, and they are likely to spread to many more American cities in the near future.

Understanding Homelessness

The chronically homeless, those who live on the streets permanently rather than those who are sporadically in and out of homes, have consistently presented the most difficult problem for cities to solve. As Kevin Fagan, a *San Francisco Chronicle* reporter who from 2003 to 2006 was the only journalist in the country writing exclusively about homelessness, told the HPR, the chronically homeless make up between 10 and 40 percent of a city's street population, and virtually all are mentally ill or addicted to drugs or alcohol. They survive relying solely on their ability to scrounge for food, get their next fix, and find a safe stoop to sleep on each night. There is a strong focus on getting this population off the streets; according to Fagan, "if you help the worst-hit segments of the homelessness problem, it frees up resources to help the rest of the homeless population." If cities can find a viable solution to the hardest problem, other urban issues become easier to tackle.

The economic crisis has certainly had adverse effects on efforts to slow homelessness. Mary Brosnahan, Executive Director for the Coalition of the Homeless, describes the problem as "a revolving door" of Americans moving in and out of homelessness. In the 1990s, at least 2.3 million people, and perhaps as many as 3.5 million people, experienced homelessness at some point, annually. The housing crisis has only exacerbated this problem. Ironically, however, the crisis does not significantly affect the chronically homeless population—

without jobs or homes, they are largely unaffected by rising unemployment and foreclosures. Yet the problem remains dire. The Interagency Council's "Ten-Year Plans" signal a shift from "service to solving," according to Mangano, and have brought significant success to the cities that implement them.

Ten-Year Plans

Representatives of the Interagency Council have traveled the country promoting these "Ten-Year Plans," influencing cities to put greater political will and resources into fighting homelessness than ever before. According to Mangano, these plans are "field tested and evidence-based," and locally constructed in each community, "not shaped inside the Beltway [of Washington, D.C.]" They are initiated, led, and managed by local mayors and county officials who bring together community stakeholders to craft specific plans.

One source of the plans' success, Mangano asserts, is their business-like models. "If there's one thing we've learned in the last 25 years, it's that if well-meaning programs could end homelessness, it would have been over years ago," he noted. Rather than relying on moral, spiritual, or humanitarian arguments, the plans look at economic cost studies. For example, it has been calculated that, while it costs between $35,000 and $150,000 in police monitoring and medical costs to leave one chronically homeless person on the street for a year, it only costs $13,000 to $25,000 per year to give that same person housing and counseling. In the United States, an emergency room visit costs $1000 on average, an ambulance ride $500. Costs like this add up quickly, and the homeless have no insurance to cover them. As Fagan found in his reporting, one particular woman in San Francisco cost upwards of $100,000 of taxpayer money a year to live on the street. As Mangano says, "you don't need to be [billionaire] Warren Buffet or [financial expert] Suze Orman to know which of those investments makes sense." The U.S. Interagency Council on Homelessness recently published some encouraging financial numbers: efforts by Seattle/King County's Eastlake Housing First program have saved the city $4 million, and Massachusetts's Housing First pilot program has shown a 67 percent reduction in annual health care costs per person. These numbers often prove far more persuasive than moral arguments in convincing mayors to implement the plans.

Nonetheless, some experts argue that the "Ten-Year Plans" focus too much on the already homeless and not enough on systems—such as healthcare, education, and social services—which must be reformed in order to truly end homelessness. As Dr. Kedar Karki, author, sociologist, and homelessness activist, told the HPR, "When assistance is restricted to those who are homeless tonight, not much can be done to prevent homelessness tomorrow." Mangano agrees that reforms are needed in other areas, but holds firm that "affordable housing [for those who are homeless now] is the most important public policy evolution that needs to take place."

Seeing Is Believing

Mangano's approach has certainly had a significant impact. From 2005 to 2007, 350 local "Ten-Year Plans" in cities throughout the country brought a 30 percent decrease in chronic homelessness. This statistic translates into 52,000 people leaving the streets and finding housing. While the economic downturn has produced an increase in overall homelessness, chronic homelessness—the crux of the problem—is decreasing. As long as this trend continues, we will see more and more cities implementing "Ten-Year Plans" and adopting the new philosophy that a solution to homelessness is possible.

Periodical Bibliography

The following articles have been selected to supplement the diverse views presented in this chapter.

Ronald Bailey — "Is Crime Contagious?," *Reason*, November 25, 2008.

Kevin Boyle — "Requiem: Detroit and the Fate of Urban America," *Origins*, May 2009.

Peter Edelman — "The Next War on Poverty," *Democracy*, Winter 2010.

Matt Harvey — "Slums of Detroit: A Look at the Heart of America's 2nd Most Deserted City," *eXiled*, December 14, 2009.

Ron Haskins — "Family Matters: Improving Inner-City Neighborhoods," Brookings Institution, Spring 2010. www.brookings.edu.

Candice Kountz and Isabel Kaplan — "Ending the Shootout," *Harvard Political Review*, May 24, 2009.

Frank Kovarik — "Mapping the Divide," *St. Louis Magazine*, December 2008.

Heather Mac Donald — "Bribery Strikes Out," *City Journal*, Summer 2010.

Sarah More McCann — "Wanted: Inner-City Supermarkets," *Christian Science Monitor*, July 27, 2008.

Cait Murphy — "Waking Up in a City of Second Chances," *Crain's New York Business*, June 28, 2010.

Nathan Thornburgh — "Crime: Looking for a Few Good Snitches," *Time*, February 19, 2006.

William Julius Wilson — "More than Just Race: Being Black and Poor in the Inner City," *Poverty & Race*, May/June 2009.

OPPOSING
VIEWPOINTS®
SERIES

CHAPTER 2

What Government Programs Would Improve Urban America?

Chapter Preface

One in eight Americans—a record 39.68 million individuals—were receiving food stamps in February 2010, according to the US Department of Agriculture (USDA). This figure represents a jump of 260,000 from the previous month. The USDA estimates that by the fall of 2011, 43.3 million people will be enrolled in the program, which is currently called the Supplemental Nutrition Assistance Program (SNAP). "The food stamp program, the first line of defense against hunger and undernutrition in the U.S., is a critically important but underutilized resource for urban America," declares the Food Research and Action Center (FRAC). Its 2006 report indicated that approximately half of qualified households were not receiving these benefits in major cities such as Los Angeles, Las Vegas, and Seattle. "Underparticipation in the food stamp program adversely affects not only low-income people who are missing out on benefits," contends FRAC, "but also communities that could be benefiting from more federal dollars circulating in the local economy." Moreover, FRAC insists that "food insecurity and hunger are more severe in America's urban centers."[1]

Critics, however, argue that the food stamp program must be reformed to eliminate fraud. "America is entirely too loose with its money, and its new immigrants know it," says Matt Hayes, a former immigration lawyer. "As recent raids and prosecutions have shown, greater oversight of programs like the one that makes food stamps readily available to new immigrants is crucial,"[2] he says. Others allege that food stamps are outright counterproductive. "Obesity is a problem for the poor in America . . . food insufficiency is not," argues Megan

1. Quoted in MyFoodStamps.org, "Food Stamp Access in Urban America: A City-by-City Snapshot," October 2006. www.myfoodstamps.org/pdf_files/FRACcities06.pdf.
2. Quoted at Fox News, November 27, 2002. www.foxnews.com/story/0,2933,72137,00.html.

McArdle, business and economics editor for the *Atlantic*. She adds, "Food stamps only imperfectly translate into increased cash income, meaning that the poor will spend . . . more money on food."[3] In the following chapter, the authors debate the benefits and consequences of government programs for helping urban America.

---

3. *www.theatlantic.com*, January 24, 2008, http://www.theatlantic.com/business/archive/2008/01/why-not-food-stamps/2613/

| "Mixed-income communities [are successful] as a strategy to deconcentrate poverty, create more culturally diverse communities, positively impact school equity, and create a more financially viable public housing."

Mixed-Income Public Housing Improves Urban America

Charles Woodyard

In the following viewpoint, Charles Woodyard asserts that the federal Housing for People Everywhere (HOPE VI) program, an initiative of the US Department of Housing and Urban Development, helps to eliminate urban blight and to disperse concentrations of poverty by replacing distressed public housing with mixed-income units. Woodyard attests that the program in Charlotte, North Carolina, transformed the site of a crime-ridden housing complex and surrounding areas into a diverse, thriving neighborhood with a wide range of incomes. For low-income families, HOPE VI served as a stepping stone away from govern-

Charles Woodyard, written testimony of Charles Woodyard, president/CEO of the Charlotte Housing Authority, submitted to the U.S. House of Representatives Committee on Financial Services, Subcommittee for Housing and Community Opportunity, June 21, 2007. Reprinted with permission.

ment assistance to self-sufficiency and a better quality of life, he contends. Woodyard is the president and chief executive officer of the Charlotte Housing Authority.

As you read, consider the following questions:

1. What does HOPE VI attempt to do for America's economy and citizens, according to the author?

2. In Woodyard's view, how does the mixed-income approach to building communities benefit public housing residents?

3. How does the Charlotte Housing Authority manage gentrification, as stated by the author?

The HOPE VI [Housing for People Everywhere] program's original mandate of eliminating distressed units of public housing across the nation and replacing them with mixed-income communities represents a formidable task. Add to that task the additional goal of deconcentrating poverty plus eliminating urban blight and you have a complicated public policy goal that impacts real people and the health of America's cities. To the extent that cities are a collection of commercial economies that thrive or suffer as a result of market forces and government intervention, HOPE VI can be seen as an attempt to grow and stabilize America's economy. To the extent that cities are a collection of diverse people, diverse cultures and children who are the foundation of the country's future, HOPE VI can be seen as an attempt to raise the minimum standard of living for more Americans.

Whatever your take on HOPE VI as a public policy might be, it is important to understand that public policy must also have a measurable impact on the lives of Americans and the health of American communities.

With this in mind, it would be helpful to understand the nature of Charlotte, NC and how HOPE VI is used as a growth strategy, a community building strategy and a way to impact the self-sufficiency efforts of very low-income families. Charlotte is a growing Sunbelt city of over 650,000. Its real estate market is among the most vibrant in the country, unemployment is low, home prices are rising rapidly despite the national trend, but income increases are not quite keeping pace with housing and energy cost increases. The result is that over 11,000 very low-income families in the community either live in substandard housing or pay more than 30% of their income for housing. Charlotte is suffering from growing pains.

The city also recognizes that housing development patterns are at the heart of school equity issues, economic development, transportation, and race relations. In order for Charlotte to grow while avoiding some of the more common growth pitfalls, the city has adopted smart growth policies that include light rail and transit oriented development, incentives for infill development, and is currently considering land use strategies that disperse affordable housing around the city.

A major catalyst for the idea of a new way of providing affordable housing as a growth strategy was the city's first HOPE VI grant. Earle Village was a 400-plus unit public housing complex in the heart of uptown Charlotte. This low-income housing community dominated an entire quadrant of the uptown area and was the major source of crime, the perception of crime, the lack of housing development in uptown and the suppression of property values in the uptown. The award of the city's first HOPE VI grant meant that mixed-income housing and mixed-use development would be the norm for infill development. The HOPE VI site was transformed into a diverse community with different housing types, incomes nearly along the entire spectrum of incomes. The impact was not limited to the Earle Village site. The onslaught of economic development in Charlotte's center city can be traced directly to the HOPE VI grant. The next logical question then, is what happened to all those families in Earle Village and other families in HOPE VI communities?

HOPE VI in Charlotte

The Charlotte Housing Authority (CHA) has received four HOPE VI revitalization grants and one demolition grant for a total of over $122 million. The Federal Government's HOPE VI investment has leveraged and/or stimulated over $750 million in private investment plus over $35 million in local government funds. As impressive as those dollar figures are, they are almost incidental to the real story behind the numbers.

The five communities directly impacted by the HOPE VI grants totaled 1531 units of severely distressed, crime ridden apartment homes that were breeding grounds for social disorder. The HOPE VI grants eliminated those distressed communities and replaced them with thirteen mixed-income family communities, five public housing senior communities, and 474 Section 8 vouchers. These new communities contain 1366 public housing units, 974 moderate income affordable rental units, 978 market rate rental units, and 85 homeownership units developed on the original HOPE VI sites for former public housing families. All totaled, 1531 housing opportunities for 30% AMI [area median income] and below families were transformed into 1729 housing opportunities in mixed-income environments or Section 8 vouchers in neighborhoods of their choice.

Additionally, the physical environments of the newly constructed apartment units and homeownership units were a vast improvement over the dilapidated public housing communities they replaced. Rental units for public housing residents in mixed-income communities are indistinguishable from market rate units and have all of the amenities associated with an "A" property. The mixed-income approach to community building has allowed public housing residents to mitigate the stigma of public housing, model their behavior after their mainstream neighbors, and move into economic self-sufficiency at a rate that would not have happened without the financial stimulus provided by the HOPE VI grants.

Quality of Life

While cautioning that steep barriers remain firmly in place for the poorest Americans, housing advocates are cautiously endorsing Hope VI's first decade. "Thus far, research indicates that mixed-income public-housing developments can be successful in creating well-managed communities that attract higher-income tenants," the Urban Institute reported. Enumerating and assessing the broad community impacts that the program aims for is a complex task, but among the studies examined by the Urban Institute, it is already clear that projects around the country have leveraged the investment to catalyze new parks, libraries, and police stations, as well as banks, restaurants, and supermarkets. Other research reveals improvements in the quality of life in neighborhoods where Hope VI projects have been built, including per-capita income increases, drops in unemployment and crime, and downward shifts in the concentration of poverty. Economic indicators, such as rates of lending and mortgage originations, have been shown to rise.

Rachel Peterson, SPUR Newsletter, *March 2005.*

Furthermore, the Charlotte Housing Authority has utilized mixed-income communities as a strategy to deconcentrate poverty, create more culturally diverse communities, positively impact school equity, and create a more financially viable public housing stock.

Growing Pains

According to our own local research, the affordable housing problem in Charlotte impacts low-income families more than any other income level. The need for 11,000 additional units in Charlotte for families earning at or below 30% AMI (Area Median Income) is the only income level in the city that demonstrates a shortage of units. In a city with this demography, one for one replacement is essential public policy. Charlotte's Housing Authority is subjected to tremendous local pressure to commit to one for one replacement when revitalizing a community under HOPE VI. As a part of our latest HOPE VI initiative, we are on track to replace more units for 30% AMI families than originally existed at the public housing site.

Another determining factor in one for one replacement is the careful management of gentrification. By its very nature, the HOPE VI program promotes gentrification. However, managing gentrification so that it maintains the delicate balance between stabilization and diversity versus the complete displacement of low-income families requires careful attention. In Charlotte, residents are given a priority for moving back into the revitalized community. However, we do require that residents commit to pursuing genuine efforts at attaining self-sufficiency.

Relocated Residents

The experience for relocated residents in surrounding neighborhoods utilizing housing choice vouchers has been positive. The majority of residents requesting relocation with housing choice vouchers want the opportunity to select the future neighborhood in which they will reside. The flexibility of the voucher program has aided in deconcentrating low income residents from a concentrated area and improved the quality of housing. The resident utilization of housing choice vouchers for relocation from the first HOPE VI in 1992 at Earle Village was 53 vouchers compared to the last HOPE VI in 2004 at Piedmont Courts which was 158 vouchers. This represents a 198% increase for the use of Section 8 vouchers and proves that housing vouchers are the preferred relocation method for residents. The majority of CHA families have a seamless transition to surrounding neighborhoods. . . .

Resident Screening

The Charlotte Housing Authority has committed itself to the goal of assisting its residents in their pursuit of self-sufficiency. In the early 1990's, CHA began its "Campaign for Self-Sufficiency." As a part of the overall campaign, CHA implemented a number of programs designed to aid residents in ending welfare dependency and poor quality of life. These programs include the Family Self-Sufficiency program, the Bootstrap/Homeless Program, the Family Unification Program, the Gateway to Family Self-Sufficiency, the Stepping Stone program, and the HOPE VI program. Under the auspices of four HOPE VI grants received by CHA for Earle Village, Dalton Village, Fairview Homes and Piedmont Courts, residents of these communities are being offered the benefits of these programs with the additional support of funding to provide tuition assistance, childcare subsidies, and other funding as needed to support the goal of self-sufficiency.

The Campaign for Family Self-Sufficiency ensures that public housing is a vehicle for families to obtain the skills and training necessary for entry into the private marketplace and a "stepping stone" to get off public assistance and out of public housing. The Campaign is part of the Transitional Families Program, started by CHA to promote self-sufficiency and economic independence among public housing residents. Authorized by the 1987 Housing Act as the Transitional Families Demonstration Program, the Transitional Families Program (TFP) has been established as an overall umbrella organization to promote self-sufficiency for all programs operated by CHA. Families who participate in a self-sufficiency program are expected to move out of public housing and into the private market within five (5) years. . . .

Tremendous Potential

To say that HOPE VI has been a success in Charlotte would be an understatement by many measures. However, other cities have duplicated this success and many more could with the appropriate changes to the program. . . .

HOPE VI has tremendous potential to continue changing the American landscape. The model for public housing must change and we must all adopt new paradigms for solving this country's affordable housing crisis. Mixed-income housing is a proven winner.

*"The 'mixed income' residency require-
ment causes the poorest of the tenants—those most in need of subsidies—to lose their homes."*

Mixed-Income Public Housing Has Not Improved Urban America

James Tracy

*In the following viewpoint, James Tracy argues that the federal
Housing Opportunities for People Everywhere (HOPE VI) program, which supports the building of mixed-income residences to
replace existing housing projects, displaces the urban poor. The
author alleges that the HOPE VI program significantly decreases
the number of public housing units available to low-income tenants because the program does not require that affordable units
be replaced on a one-to-one basis. Moreover, he contends that
the program's aim to deconcentrate areas of poverty ignores the
problems of unemployment and racism and breaks up the political power of poor communities. Tracy is an adult education in-
structor at the Community Housing Partnership, a board member of the San Francisco Community Land Trust, and a writer.*

James Tracy, "Hope VI Mixed-Income Housing Projects Displace Poor People," *Race,
Poverty & the Environment: Who Owns the City?* vol. 15, Spring 2008. Reproduced by
permission of the author.

As you read, consider the following questions:

1. As told by the author, what happened to the Techwood Housing Project under HOPE VI?

2. Why does mixed-income housing make exiting homelessness through public housing impossible, in Tracy's view?

3. How does HOPE VI result in "urban removal," according to the author?

If you have ever lived in or around a public housing development you would probably agree with the stated aim of the federal Housing Opportunities for People Everywhere (HOPE VI) program: Drastic measures are needed to improve the dilapidated buildings and uplift the lives of the people who live in them.

HOPE VI provides grant money from the United States Department of Housing and Urban Development (HUD) to local housing authorities to demolish and reconstruct "distressed" projects. Tenants receive relocation assistance and a portable Section 8 voucher to subsidize their rent in the private market while their public housing developments are demolished—entirely or in part—and reconstructed as mixed-income housing complexes in an attempt to deconcentrate pockets of intense poverty.

In theory, the original tenants are then able to return to their refurbished homes and enjoy a wide range of social and economic programs designed to ease the transition from welfare to work. In reality, what often happens is that the reconstruction is delayed or abandoned altogether, or the "mixed income" residency requirement causes the poorest of the tenants—those most in need of subsidies—to lose their homes.

A Brief History of HOPE

Since 1992, HUD has awarded 446 HOPE VI grants in 166 cities. As of 2006, 78,100 public housing units had been demolished, and an additional 10,400 units were slated for redevelopment.

However, a 2004 study by the Urban Institute found that only 21,000 units had been built to replace the 49,828 demolished units. In other words, roughly 42 percent of the demolished public housing had been replaced.

In 1940, President [Franklin D.] Roosevelt stood in front of Atlanta's Techwood Housing Project, the first completed federally funded public housing, and said, "Within a very short time people who never before could get a decent roof over their heads will live here in reasonable comfort and healthful, worthwhile surroundings."

In 1996, despite its special place in history, the Techwood Project was the first to be demolished under HOPE VI to make room for the Olympic village. However, visitors to the Olympics were still able to walk through a virtual reality exhibit of Techwood, but without the annoying presence of its displaced tenants. The original Techwood contained 1100 units—all of them for public housing. Today, only 300 units are available for public housing.

A HOPE Based on Punishment

Under the [Bill] Clinton and [George W.] Bush administrations, Republicans and Democrats have colluded to systematically dismantle what was left of the social welfare system ushered in by the New Deal. Throughout the 1990s, the rhetoric of welfare reform blamed "cultures of poverty" and "concentrations of poverty" for poverty itself. Instead of getting tough on corporate layoffs of thousands of people during peak profit time, Clinton decided to show "tough love" to those most likely to be at the receiving end of structural unemployment.

Of course, it would be a grave mistake to stereotype all public housing residents as welfare recipients because public housing tenants are often some of the hardest working but poorest paid people. In 1999, the median income of families living in public housing was $6,500, well below a living wage by any standard. In their essay "Failing, but Not Fooling, Public Housing Residents," authors Jacqueline Leavitt and Mary Ochs point out that both "welfare reform" and "public housing reform," take a punitive approach to public policy and make false assumptions about the availability of decent-paying jobs and adequate job training. Interestingly, punishment and privatization often seem to go hand-in-hand.

In 1996, President Clinton signed into law a bill designed to accelerate evictions in public housing. Dubbed "One Strike and You're Out," it was touted as a way to stop drug trafficking and violent crimes in public housing developments. Since One Strike was a civil procedure, tenants could be evicted even if they were acquitted of criminal charges. In effect, what One Strike did was provide an excuse for eviction based solely on innuendo and allegations of criminal activity. Thankfully, in January 2001, the Ninth Circuit Court of Appeals eliminated those provisions of "One Strike," which allowed evictions of those who were both innocent and ignorant of the crime for which they were being evicted.

Resisting HOPE

In 1996, a small group of residents at a North Beach public housing facility in San Francisco who were concerned about being displaced by HOPE VI decided to fight back. They sought the help of the Eviction Defense Network (EDN), which had previously led a successful campaign to prevent evictions of undocumented residents.

There followed a three-year, door-to-door campaign of organizing and educating the tenants about the dangers of relocating for HOPE VI upgrades without a firm promise of a home to return to. Consequently, more than 60 percent of the tenants signed pledges not to move until they had received real guarantees. The San Francisco Housing Authority (SFHA), fearing that delays and a failure to comply with HUD mandates would cause them to lose $23 million in HOPE VI money, relented. The tenants were offered an "Exit Contract" with legally binding guarantees, most significant among them: one-for-one replacement of all demolished low-income units and a limited number of reasons for disqualifying a tenant from re-occupancy. Charged by this modest victory, the tenant activists of North Beach drafted a Public Housing Tenant Protection Act (PHTPA) as a citywide ordinance. Although supported by San Francisco Board Of Supervisors President Tom Ammiano, and passed by the Finance and Labor Committee, the measure was eventually killed by Supervisor Amos Brown.

No Hope for the Homeless

The Quality Housing and Work Responsibility Act (QHWRA) of 1998 mandates that all public housing developments should become "mixed income," meaning, all new housing units are for those making 30 to 80 percent of the median income. In effect, this makes it virtually impossible to exit homelessness via the public housing system.

Partnerships with the private sector are key in reducing federal government costs for low-income housing. According to HOPE VI proponents, the average annual direct costs are reduced by $3.9 million for public housing units redeveloped as mixed-income housing. But urban land being at a premium, the HOPE VI process usually results in the privatization of many developments as developers contracted to do the reconstruction generally gain partial ownership (currently estimated at around one billion dollars) of the new housing. So, the poor continue to lose, as corporations, such as McCormack Baron, Sun America, and Bridge Housing Developers make immense profit.

Nationwide, there are now over one million families awaiting subsidized housing (as acknowledged by HUD's own research) but the federal government continues to cut back on available units.

Political Diffusion

The United States Code of Federal Regulations has identified "the growth of population in metropolitan and other urban areas, and the concentration of persons of lower income in central cities" and set a goal to "develop new centers of population growth and economic activity." Its apparent objective is "the reduction of the isolation of income groups within communities and geographical areas and the promotion and increase in the diversity and vitality of neighborhoods through the spatial deconcentration of housing opportunities of persons of lower income and the revitalization of deteriorating neighborhoods."

In other words, poverty is a result of poor people living in close proximity to each other—rather than of structural unemployment or the persistence of racism—and "economic integration," or living close to employed people will set a good example for the poor.

Is spatial deconcentration a progressive solution to poverty or a hideous experiment in social engineering? One obvious effect of spatial deconcentration is the dilution of the political power wielded by concentrated voting blocks. The other is that it makes more difficult any political organizing for the common economic interests of a community.

Author Yolanda Ward traces the theoretical roots of spatial deconcentration to when President Lyndon Johnson established the National Advisory Commission on Civil Disorders commonly known as the Kerner Commission. Inner city riots were frequent in the 1960s. (San Francisco's largest was in 1966—a community response to the police killing of Matthew Johnson, a 16-year-old African American youth from the Bayview [neighborhood].) The Commission was set up to investigate the origins of 160 disorders in 128 cities in the first nine months of 1967.

The Kerner Commission report, released in 1968, recommended traditional liberal solutions to poverty, such as strengthening the social safety net and increasing job opportunities for inner-city citizens. It also suggested spatial deconcentration as a viable strategy to deter urban uprisings.

Whatever the intentions of its promoters, the end result of spatial deconcentration (supported by the [Richard] Nixon, [Ronald] Reagan, [George] Bush Sr. and Jr., and Clinton administrations) has been the political demobilization of the oppressed as poor residents are scattered to the suburbs.

Pushing the Poor Out of Town

Urban Habitat studies published in the 1990s track the deconcentration process in the Bay Area where displaced low-income residents generally are dispersed to the rim cities of Antioch, Vallejo, San Pablo, Dixon, El Cerrito, and Vacaville. In each of these areas, the number of available jobs exceeds the population. Some, like Vallejo and Alameda, have suffered high unemployment rates as a result of military base closures. So, public housing transplants to these areas often have to commute to the metropolitan areas to find low-wage work.

Overt political racism is another issue that gentrification refugees have to face in the rim cities. A case in point is the early morning raid conducted by a Vallejo city taskforce on the federally subsidized but privately owned Marina Green development in 1997. Over 60 families were rousted from their beds and forced to watch as officers ransacked their apartments for no apparent reason other than that they all received welfare.

The irony of federal housing policy "reform" is that it uses a progressive critique to accomplish completely conservative aims. The HOPE VI program argues against warehousing the

Cost of "Affordable Housing"

One must . . . question the cost of producing "affordable housing" in the HOPE VI project when compared to other nonprofit urban housing efforts. Comparisons show that the cost of producing one housing unit is two to three times higher for the HOPE VI developments than for comparable community-controlled nonprofits. During the same time period as the HOPE VI project, the nonprofit Louisville Central Development Corporation was able to build units for as low as $49,500 for a three-bedroom, one full-bath apartment. These units were attractive and were within walking distance of downtown high-wage jobs, shopping, entertainment, and recreational activities. They were constructed on sites adjacent to middle-income homeowners. Altogether, nonprofit organizations provided approximately 100 of these units at a very low cost. Compare this to the $54,232,667 spent on [HOPE-financed] Park DuValle to date, producing 320 residential units at a cost of $169,000 per unit.

Michael Brazley and John I. Gilderbloom,
American Journal of Economics and Sociology, *April 2007.*

poor in substandard areas, and many housing authorities actually have self-sufficiency programs for their residents to prepare for gainful employment. However, by abolishing the requirement that demolished public housing units be replaced on a one-for-one basis and cutting funding, Congress has effectively given the federal government an exit strategy out of the public housing business.

As the nationwide housing crisis intensifies and the nation teeters on the brink of a recession, we are faced with the type of economic and political conditions that existed during the

Great Depression. We can only hope that they will lead to a re-emergence of some of the more enlightened and progressive social programs of that era.

Legacy of Destruction

The term "urban removal" refers explicitly to the government-financed-and-facilitated destruction of inner-city housing. In the case of HOPE VI, the destruction is of government-owned developments but in some cases, the government also seized private property and removed entire communities.

The Western Addition or Fillmore District of San Francisco is ground zero in the history of urban removal. The first removal in that area occurred with the internment of Japanese-American citizens during World War II. The area was then populated by Blacks who were aggressively recruited from the southern states to work in the Bay Area building war machines. During the war years, Blacks not only enjoyed a degree of economic prosperity, the neighborhood became a center for jazz, blues, and the arts. But when the war ended, the government started a propaganda campaign against the Fillmore, branding it "blighted." Given the relative prosperity of the Fillmore at the time, the notion of "blight" had little to do with decrepit conditions, but everything to do with racist assumptions and developer profit.

The urban renewal legislation passed by Congress in 1949 and 1954 conferred Redevelopment Agencies with the power to condemn entire city blocks and evict residents, be they renters or owners. The process of eminent domain proved devastating to the roughly 17,000 people displaced during both phases of the project.

Before urban removal, a large portion of Blacks owned their own homes. Joyce Miller was nine years old when her family was forced to leave their home under the threat of eminent domain. "They offered the families some money, usually less than what the place was worth," Miller recalls. "They told you that if you didn't accept, they would take your home anyhow."

Although Miller's family found housing not far from their former home, other residents were not as lucky. "The realtors made sure that if you stayed in San Francisco, you went only to the Ingleside District or the Bayview," she says. "Everyone else was pushed out of the city."

| "Rail transit is exactly the type of service that can provide travel time savings and user comfort on congested urban corridors."

Urban Rail Transit Benefits Cities

Todd Litman

In the following viewpoint, Todd Litman argues that urban rail transit is advantageous where transportation demand is high, compact development is desirable, and congestion from buses would cause problems of pollution and noise. Furthermore, Litman states rail transit supports economic development by cutting the costs and liabilities of traffic, encouraging more-efficient land use, and reducing dependency on oil, which shifts consumer spending to the local economy. Buses may cost less to operate, but the author contends that the quality of service is inferior. Litman is founder and executive director of the Victoria Transport Policy Institute in Victoria, British Columbia, Canada.

As you read, consider the following questions:

1. How does Litman counter the argument that rail transit development is a "war on suburbs"?

Todd Litman, "Evaluating Rail Transit Criticism," pp. 24–31, Victoria Transit Policy Institute, 2010. Reproduced by permission.

2. How would rail transit benefit San Antonio, Texas, according to the author?

3. Why do commuters prefer high-quality, if slower, rail transit over driving, in Litman's view?

Critics often argue that buses can provide comparable service quality more cheaply than rail, but this is often untrue. Rail transit generally has lower operating costs per passenger-mile than bus service.... Basic bus systems generally have lower capital costs than rail, because they lack features such as grade separation, attractive stations and local pedestrian improvements. As a result, basic bus transit systems provide inferior quality service, attract fewer discretionary travelers, do less to stimulate transit-oriented development, and therefore provide smaller benefits than rail transit systems. As bus service is improved to achieve these benefits, with grade separation and nicer stations, its costs tend to increase toward that of rail.

Rail and bus each have advantages and disadvantages, so each is suitable for certain situations. Rail tends to provide faster service, more comfortable vehicles and stations, better integration with other modes and land use, and more prestige than buses. Rail is therefore most appropriate on major corridors where demand is high, where compact development is desirable, and where heavy bus traffic would cause noise and air pollution problems. Bus is most appropriate serving dispersed destinations and where transit supportive development policies cannot be implemented. Bus Rapid Transit (BRT) systems can provide some of these amenities, including grade separation, and more comfortable vehicles and stations, but this raises their costs closer to that of rail.

Critics sometimes claim that rail transit requires very high population densities (often reported at 75 residents per acre) and highrise housing, and can only serve downtowns. These are exaggerations. Rail can function efficiently with densities as low as 25 residents (about 10 housing units) per acre, which can be achieved with a combination of single-family and mid-rise multi-family housing. Rail can connect various destinations, including business districts, sports and cultural centers, campuses, shopping malls, and suburban residential areas.

A War on Cars and Suburbs?

A paper by Wendell Cox (2010) titled, *Washington's War on Cars and the Suburbs: Secretary LaHood's False Claims on Roads and Transit*, criticizes USDOT [US Department of Transportation] rail transit investment plans, claiming that rail transit benefits are unproven and exaggerated. It criticizes my report, *Rail Transit in America: Comprehensive Evaluation of Benefits*, published by the American Public Transportation Association, the source of many of the Secretary's assertions. Cox's criticisms are evaluated below. . . .

The USDOT's policy changes respond to demographic and economic trends which are increasing consumer demands for alternative modes and smart-growth communities, including aging population, rising future fuel prices, increased traffic congestion, growing health and environmental concerns, and changing consumer preference.

Cox claims that, "people are free to choose cars or transit for their travel, and the car tends to be preferred by those who can afford it." This is not true. Most US communities lack high quality transit, leading to low ridership, but as previously described, where quality transit exists its mode share is five to ten times higher than the U.S. average, indicating significant latent demand. Only if high quality transit is available can travelers choose the option that best meets their needs for each trip and indicate the true level of consumer demand for such service.

Economic Impacts

As previously described, rail transit helps support economic development in several ways: it increases overall accessibility; reduces various economic costs (traffic congestion, road and parking costs, accident damages, pollution, etc.); helps create more compact land use development that achieves agglomeration efficiencies; and shifts consumer expenditures toward goods with greater regional input; and reduces oil vulnerability and trade deficits. This helps explain why rail transit cities tend to have much higher per capita GDP [gross domestic product, a measure of economic output] than average. . . .

Cox argues that the economic benefits of rail transit are minuscule, but subsequent analysis indicates these benefits are even larger than originally estimated. *Rail Transit in America* used Input/Output analysis to quantify the increased regional employment and business activity that results when high quality transit allows consumers to shift their spending from vehicles and fuel to other goods with greater local input. Cox legitimately points out that the 1999 study used as the basis for calculating these economic impacts in *Rail Transit in America* is dated and limited because it reflects a single urban region (it was the only study of its type available at the time). However, more recent studies show similar results. As previously described, a million dollars of fuel savings shifted to a typical consumer bundle of goods adds about 4.5 jobs to the U.S. economy, a million dollars shifted from other automobile expenditures (vehicles, servicing, insurance, etc.) adds 3.6 jobs.

Consider the impacts in San Antonio, [Texas,] as Cox does. In 2005, U.S. consumers spent an average of $3,500 annually on vehicles and fuel. The San Antonio metropolitan area has about 2.0 million residents, so regional consumers spend about $7.0 billion annually on vehicles and fuel. If high quality transit can reduce these expenses 20%, as it does in other urban regions, the $1.4 billion annual consumer savings would increase domestic employment by about 5,600 jobs, with larger gains at the regional level, and these benefits should [increase] in the future as petroleum prices rise.

Of course, developing high quality transit service in San Antonio would require significant service improvements. Cox estimates that doubling San Antonio's transit ridership would require $150 million in additional annual expenditures, which seems large compared with current transit funding but is only 1–2% of current regional spending on vehicles (about $3,500 per capita, $7.0 billion total), roads (about $500 per capita, $1.0 billion total) and parking facilities (about $2,000 per capita, $4.0 billion total).

Energy Savings

Cox argues that rail provides only modest energy savings and emission reductions compared with driving a modern, fuel efficient car, based on comparisons of fuel consumption rates per passenger-mile. However, as previously discussed, this ignores the much larger energy savings and emission reductions indicated by lifecycle analysis which accounts for upstream and embodied energy, and the energy savings that result from reductions in total per capita vehicle travel. . . . Residents of transit-oriented communities typically drive 20–40% less than in automobile-dependent communities, and so consume that much less fuel. . . .

Transit Travel Time

Much of Cox's criticism is based on the assumptions that transit travel is always slower and less desirable than driving. He aggregates data, for example, by comparing overall average commute times for all transit modes (including buses in mixed traffic and longer-distance commuter rail) with driving, rather than comparing rail with driving to the same destination. Although transit tends to be slower *on average*, on major urban corridors, grade separated rail transit is often faster than driving, for example, between Brooklyn and Manhattan, Oakland and San Francisco, or Cambridge and Boston.

Even when slower, travelers often prefer high quality transit because they can use their travel time productively (to work, read or rest), it is less stressful than driving, and they enjoy the walking links of transit trips. For example, New Jersey train commuters report less stress and fewer negative moods than auto commuters. Similarly, a U.K. survey found that many rail passengers use their travel time for working (30% sometimes and 13% most times), reading (54% sometimes and 34% most times), resting (16% sometimes and 4% most times) and talking (15% sometimes and 5% most times), particularly during business travel.

Cox summarily dismisses the possibility that transit travel is ever more productive or preferable to driving. He states, "Riders of the nation's largest rail transit systems (such as the New York subway and the Chicago El) routinely encounter overcrowded conditions during peak periods, with riders forced to stand." This is wrong. Although a portion of peak-period rail passengers stand, overall most transit passengers have seats.

This is not to suggest that everybody prefers transit for all trips, but high quality, grade separated rail transit is exactly the type of service that can provide travel time savings and user comfort on congested urban corridors. If such service is available, travelers can choose the best mode for each trip: transit for some and driving for others. This increases user benefits, and by reducing traffic problems, provides external benefits. Cox's criticism therefore supports rail transit improvements to increase user and social benefits.

"Building rail transit in a city becomes a cancer to normal, sustainable activity, as that rail line becomes a growing burden."

Urban Rail Transit Does Not Benefit Cities

Randal O'Toole

Randal O'Toole is a senior fellow at the Cato Institute and author of The Best-Laid Plans: How Government Planning Harms Your Quality of Life, Your Pocketbook, and Your Future. *In the following viewpoint, O'Toole argues against the development of urban rail for several reasons. He contends that rail lines are much more expensive than buses and highway systems and that the enormous energy costs offset the energy savings. Also, rail transit agencies never collect enough fares to cover operating costs, O'Toole contends, which diverts funds and cuts other transportation services. Finally, he warns that rail transit agencies monopolize land use so that jobs and homes end up being near rail stations.*

Randal O'Toole, "Urban Rail Transit: On the Wrong Track," *MasterResource* blog, April 21, 2010. www.masterresource.org. Reproduced by permission of the author.

As you read, consider the following questions:

1. According to O'Toole, what is behind the huge lobby for rail construction?

2. How does the energy consumed by a transit system per passenger mile increase because of a new rail line, in the author's view?

3. Why does a new rail line increase housing costs and job losses, in O'Toole's opinion?

In 2006, Nashville began operating the Music City Star, a commuter train between Lebanon [Tennessee] and Nashville. Transit officials brag that this is "the most cost-effective commuter train in the country" because they spent only $41 million to begin service.

To be cost-effective, however, you need more than just a train: that train needs to produce something. The Music City Star carries only about 250 commuters on round trips each day, riders who could easily have been accommodated in a few buses costing less than $3 million. In fact, it would have been less expensive to give each of those commuters a new Toyota Prius every year for the next 30 years than to operate the train.

Since 1970, American cities have spent about $100 billion building new rail transit lines, and virtually all of it has been wasted. Rail transit was rendered obsolete in the 1920s by the development of reliable buses that could go on any streets open to automobile traffic. Since the cost of the streets was shared with autos and trucks, the capital and maintenance requirements for buses are far lower than for rails.

After 1920, some 700 American cities with streetcar or other rail transit systems converted those mostly private systems to buses. By 1970, only eight urban areas still had some form of rail transit. Today, rail transit can be found in more than 30 urban areas, and the number is growing. This turnaround is largely due to perverse incentives in federal transportation funding that rewards transit agencies for selecting high-cost transit solutions when low-cost solutions—usually buses—would work better.

Predictably, the rail construction boom has generated a huge lobby for more federal funding for rail transit. The American Public Transportation Association, whose members include numerous construction and engineering firms, has a $20 million annual budget, which is several times greater than the annual budgets of all of the various highway groups in Washington combined. Most contractors that can build highways can make even more profits building rail lines, so they have no interest in opposing rail.

Three Energy Costs

One of the big arguments for building rail transit is that it will save energy. But, as I found two years ago [in 2008] in a Cato [Institute] report, the energy saved by using steel wheels instead of rubber tires is offset by three energy costs.

First, for safety reasons, rail cars must be very heavy, typically weighing 50 tons. Since rail cars carry an average of about 25 people, this means an average weight of about 4,000 pounds per person. That's more than twice the weight-per-passenger ratio of the average automobile.

Second, constructing rail lines consumes a huge amount of energy, and if those lines are lightly used the energy cost per passenger will be much higher than for highways, which are typically much more heavily used. Portland [Oregon] estimated that the energy cost of constructing one of its light-rail lines was 172 times the annual energy savings.

Third, rail transit rarely operates by itself, and instead is typically supplemented by shuttle buses that are supposed to feed passengers into the rail stations. But those buses tend to be very lightly used, while the rail lines themselves have taken passengers away from corridor bus routes that tend to be

Metropolitan Mobility

American metropolitan areas are the world's most mobile by virtue of their high levels of automobile ownership and generally superior urban roadways. This mobility, in turn, helps to make America's metropolitan areas the most productive in the world. The Organisation for Economic Co-operation and Development found that the 12 metropolitan areas with the highest GDP [gross domestic product] per capita were in the United States and that 22 of the 25 metropolitan areas with the highest GDP per capita were in the United States. People choose to commute by car because, considering all factors, including safety, greater mobility improves their standard of living.

Wendell Cox, Heritage Foundation Special Report, June 17, 2010.

heavily used. The net result is the energy consumed by a transit system per passenger mile sometimes actually increases after the system opens a new rail line.

The Data on Rail Lines

Rail advocates love to point to cities such as Portland as examples of success stories. So I gathered data on almost every rail line in the country to see if any of them could be judged successful by any objective criteria. As detailed in a recent Cato Institute report:

- None of them collects enough fares to cover their operating costs, much less any of their capital costs. New York City subway fares cover just 67 percent of operating costs, more than any other rail system.

- Almost all of them cost far more than it would have cost to provide equivalent service using buses. The only exceptions were a few commuter-rail systems in dense urban areas including Los Angeles, San Francisco, and Washington.

- Many cities spent so much money on a few rail lines that they were forced to cut funding to buses, contributing to a net loss in transit riders. Atlanta and Los Angeles, for example, practiced "transit apartheid," building rail lines into middle-class neighborhoods while cutting bus service to low-income, minority neighborhoods.

- Even where ridership has increased, it has rarely kept up with auto travel and nowhere has it reversed the trend towards suburbanization of jobs. Transit in Portland, for example, carried 9.8 percent of commuters to work before the city began building light rail; in 2007, with four light-rail lines and a streetcar line, transit carried only 6.5 percent of commuters to work.

Not only is the initial cost of rail transit high, most rail lines cost more to operate than buses and all of them cost far more to maintain. After 30 years, rail infrastructure begins to break down and must be replaced. The Washington DC rail crash that killed 9 people last June [2009] took place because that rail system is more than 30 years old and no one has provided any funds to rehabilitate it.

A Loss of Property Rights

On top of the sheer cost, rail transit usually results in a loss of property rights for many of a region's landowners. Bus routes can be easily altered in response to changing travel patterns, but rail lines cannot. So rail transit agencies often try to become land-use czars, dictating where development can take place so that new residents and jobs are located near rail stations. They try to restrict growth away from the rail lines while mandating higher-than-marketable densities in rail corridors. Cities often use tax-increment financing—effectively taking money from schools and other urban services—to promote such "transit-oriented developments."

Residents of regions that open new rail lines can expect to pay higher taxes to fund transit and even more taxes or reduced urban services to fund transit-oriented developments. They can also expect to suffer more traffic congestion as funds that might have been spent relieving congestion are spent on rail instead. Housing costs will increase as restrictions are placed on the kind of housing people want—single-family homes with a yard—while jobs may be lost as businesses move to a less heavily taxed and regulated region.

In all, building rail transit in a city becomes a cancer to normal, sustainable activity, as that rail line becomes a growing burden on legitimate transportation and even the full range of city services itself.

Periodical Bibliography

The following articles have been selected to supplement the diverse views presented in this chapter.

Keith Barrow   "Dart Takes Light Rail to the People,"
International Railway Journal, 2008.

Michelle Chen   "Urban Communities Seek Lift Through Living
Wage," *In These Times*, December 22, 2009.

Matthew Desmond   "Housing Crisis in the Inner City," *Chicago
Tribune*, April 18, 2010.

Peter Dreier   "Good Jobs, Healthy Cities," *American Prospect*,
October 19, 2009.

Yonah Freemark   "The Sprawling Effects of High-Speed Rail,"
Transport Politic, March 18, 2010.

Diana Furchtgott-Roth   "Expand New York City's Living Wage?,"
RealClearMarkets, July 1, 2010.

Peter Gertier   "Trains and the City," *Forbes*, May 5, 2009.

Jon Gertner   "What Is a Living Wage?," *New York Times*,
January 15, 2006.

S. George   "Is This the Future of Public Housing in
Louisville?," *LEO Weekly*, August 15, 2006.

Heather Knight   "Infamous Projects Are Rebuilt and Reborn,"
San Francisco Chronicle, November 20, 2006.

Peyton Miller   "Congestion Pricing," *Harvard Political Review*,
May 24, 2009.

Jeanette Wicks-Lim   "Measuring the Full Impact of Minimum and
Living Wage Laws," *Dollars & Sense*, May/June
2006.

OPPOSING
VIEWPOINTS®
SERIES

How Can the Lives of Urban Children Be Improved?

Chapter Preface

In September 2009, Derrion Albert, a sixteen-year-old honors student and football player, was killed on his way home from school in Chicago's South Side. Walking to a bus stop, he encountered a gang fight and, without provocation, several teenagers clubbed him with railroad planks. A graphic cell-phone video of the attack surfaced in news reports and stirred national outrage. As of September 2010, five youths have been charged with his murder, and they currently await trial.

The fatal beating of Derrion Albert put a human face on the crisis of youth violence in Chicago: Thirty-six public school students were murdered during the 2008–2009 school year, up five from the school year before. Albert's death also reflects an alarming trend across the country. The homicide rate of African American males between the ages of ten and twenty-four is 60.7 per 100,000, much higher than the the rate of Latinos (20.6 per 100,000) and Caucasians (3.5 per 100,000) the same age, according to the Centers for Disease Control and Prevention.

Some commentators assert that fatherlessness is an underlying cause. Reporter Kristin Gray states, "The black family is imploding."[1] Referring to a 2008 report from the US Bureau of the Census, Gray claims that African American women have the lowest rates of marriage (48 percent), compared with the marriage rates of Caucasians (69 percent) and Asian Americans (79 percent). "Needless to say, everyone involved in the Albert beating came from a fatherless home," argues Heather Mac Donald, a fellow at the Manhattan Institute. She

---

1. Kristin Gray, "African American Youth Facing Growing Threat from Peers," New America Media, October 7, 2009, http://news.newamericamedia.org/news/view_article .html?article_id=2486f2e06ce7ccbb99e80ee40b8afabc.

says, "What's lacking in these neighborhoods that we didn't notice before? The correct answer would be: family structure."[2]

Others, however, argue against such conclusions. "There is no evidence that being born in a single-parent home causes a child to become violent or become a victim of violence," says John Petro, an analyst at the Drum Major Institute for Urban Policy. He cites a recent analysis of five hundred student victims of gun violence: 7 percent were from unstable homes versus 5 percent from stable homes. "For those of us that are truly concerned with the issue of youth violence," maintains Petro, "what are the appropriate solutions? One way is to reduce the school-based factors that lead to higher levels of violence."[3] In the following chapter, the authors debate the effects and benefits of policies and programs designed to help children in urban America.

2. Heather Mac Donald, "Chicago's Real Crime Story," *City Journal*, Winter 2010. www.city-journal.org/2010/20_1_chicago-crime.html.
3. John Petro, "An Illegitimate Approach to Chicago's Youth Violence," *Huffington Post*, January 27, 2010, http://www.huffingtonpost.com/john-petro/an-illegitimate-response_b_438978.html.

| "Curfews . . . will decrease both juvenile delinquency and youth victimization."

Curfews May Reduce Crime and Protect Urban Youth

Martha Yeide

Despite the lack of research supporting the impact of curfews on juvenile crime rates, they are widely perceived as effective and enforced in a growing number of cities and urban areas, Martha Yeide argues in the following viewpoint taken from her report for the US Department of Justice. Other studies, she contends, indicate that curfews curb violent and property crimes committed by youth and may reduce juvenile trauma rates. Additionally, Yeide states that such laws may present opportunities to encourage parental involvement. The author is a research analyst for the Development Services Group in Bethesda, Maryland.

As you read, consider the following questions:

1. How does Yeide compare conservatives' support of curfews with that of liberals?

2. Why have courts upheld the right of jurisdictions to enforce curfews, in the author's words?

Martha Yeide, *Curfew Violation Literature Review*, October 15, 2009. Reproduced by permission.

3. How does Yeide back her assertion that curfew programs appear to reduce curfew violations?

In response to a wave of increasing juvenile crime in the 1980s and 1990s, many communities across the nation either implemented or began enforcing curfew statutes already on the books. In communities with age-based curfews, a violation constitutes a status offense. National figures, including President Bill Clinton, have embraced curfews as a viable way of tackling the problem of juvenile crime.

Scope of the Problem

Curfew laws can vary depending on the hours specified, the locale affected, and the age group included. In most jurisdictions, minors are required to be at home, generally between 11 p.m. and 6 a.m., though the times can vary somewhat depending on the day of the week and whether or not school is in session. Some jurisdictions apply curfew to school hours as well. Many curfew laws include exceptions for youth traveling to and from certain events (e.g., a school-, church- or civic-sponsored activity), work, or responding to emergencies.

Juvenile curfew laws have become very popular in the United States over the past 20 years. The U.S. Conference of Mayors conducted a survey in 1997 that found that 80 percent of cities surveyed had a nighttime curfew for youth. A study done in 2000 found that the rate of increase in cities with curfews was about 3 percent each year and that police have increased enforcement efforts. Reports in the popular media document the continued interest in enacting juvenile curfew laws. For instance, the City of Rochester, N.Y., implemented a curfew in September 2006. As of winter 2008 the Memphis (Tenn.) City Council was debating the need for a daytime curfew. Other communities that have had curfew laws on their books for a considerable time are either rewriting them or stepping up efforts to enforce them.

Often, curfew violators are diverted away from the juvenile justice system either through diversion programs or by receiving a warning rather than a citation. Nonetheless, a significant number of curfew violators are formally charged through the filing of a petition. According to the *Juvenile Court Statistics 2005*, the number of petitioned curfew cases increased by 61 percent between 1995 and 2000 (the cases rose from 11,900 to 19,200), but then decreased by 31 percent through 2005. Curfew violations account for 9 percent of the petitioned status offense cases in 2005, down from 10 percent in 1995.

Theoretical Contexts

Juvenile curfews laws have appealed to liberals and conservatives alike, though usually for slightly different reasons. For conservatives, curfews fit into an approach of more vigorous enforcement efforts, more punitive sentencing, and increased social controls. For liberals, curfews fit into the program of identifying juveniles in early stages of delinquency who could benefit from intervention strategies. Additionally, the costs of enforcing curfews are perceived as relatively low and the measures perceived as very effective. Little empirical research has been done on the cost-effectiveness of curfew enforcement, so this remains an area where further research would be useful.

For some, curfews appear to present an opportunity to catalyze family involvement. Comments made by those advocating for curfews make it clear that, for some, there is a connection between curfew laws and parental accountability laws. This connection was expressed as early as 1896, when Mrs. John D. Townsend commented, "[T]he curfew ordinance places responsibility where it belongs, on the parents." In 2006, as New Haven, Conn., weighed whether to enact a curfew law, Alderwoman Joyce Chen voiced regret that such measures are "the only way we're seeing now to get parents involved."

Curfew laws have been challenged on the grounds that they are unconstitutional. Arguments have been based on the curfews' violation of the following rights: freedom of speech, equal protection and due process, freedom of movement, and the right of parents to rear their children. Courts have largely held up the right of jurisdictions to impose such laws, if they meet certain legal criteria (e.g., the jurisdiction can provide data supporting that the ordinance is tailored to fulfill a public safety need). . . .

Prevention and Intervention

Although many jurisdictions have established procedures for handling curfew violators, few offer curfew programs. Of those that exist, most view curfew violations as an opportunity to offer diversion programs and services that can help families and youth avoid repeat offenses.

The SafeNite Curfew and Diversion Program, introduced in 1994 by Denver, Colo., aims to reduce the number of juvenile perpetrators and victims of crime/violence and to alleviate court congestion. Police take curfew violators who have not broken a criminal law to a SafeNite location, where they are ticketed and a background check for prior violations is conducted. Parents or guardians, who are called to the site to pick up the youth, may be cited for allowing their children to violate the ordinance if their child has received three or more citations within a short time. Youth are eligible for the diversion program based on their criminal record and the circumstances surrounding the curfew violation. Once a youth has been identified as eligible for the diversion program, the diversion officer completes an assessment of the youth that seeks to identify and address issues that may have led to the curfew violation. These issues range from a lack of knowledge about curfew to abusive home environments that have led youth to run away. Diversion plans are unique to the individual and based on the assessment. Diversion plans can include performing community service and attending work-shops on issues such as problem solving, anger management, mental health, substance abuse, and school problems. If the youth completes a specified diversion plan, no court appearance is required and the ticket is dismissed.

Camden, N.J., introduced its curfew program in 2005. The goals of the Camden City Curfew Project were to educate the community about Camden's curfew ordinance and to link young people and their families with resources including youth development programs and social services. The Project also aims to keep youth safe by removing them from public places during the hours when most violent crime occurs. Police take curfew violators to a neutral location, where youth are screened against a current violator list, an open warrant list, and a missing persons list. Parents or guardians are called to the site, where the curfew program is explained to the youth and parent. The caseworker can offer a variety of services, ranging from classes to emergency services; families also receive information about resources available in the community that can address their needs. The caseworker follows up with the family a few days later. If a youth is picked up three times, the parent or guardian is issued a *Failure to Supervise* (MC § 382-5) summons.

Evaluation Results

The rationale offered for curfews is twofold: it will decrease both juvenile delinquency and youth victimization. While many perceive the statutes as effective and cite anecdotal evidence to illustrate the efficacy of curfew statutes, most studies that have looked at the impact of curfew laws on juvenile crime have generally concluded that there is little evidence that curfew laws make a significant impact on juvenile crime rates. One study—which emphasized the methodological limitations of other studies and used a different methodological approach—suggested that curfews are effective at curbing violent and property crimes by juveniles. Research has also shown that on school days juvenile violent crime peaks in the hours following school, hours unaffected by curfew laws. On nonschool days, juvenile violent crime peaks around 8 p.m., falling quickly by 11 p.m. when most curfews take effect. Taking into consideration the number of hours in the afterschool period compared to all other hours, the rate of crime in this after school period is 6 times the rate during times covered by most curfews.

The curfew programs do appear to reduce the number of curfew violations. A report issued by the Senator Walter Rand Institute attributes the decrease in total number of juvenile arrests in Camden City from 5,076 in 2006 to 3,814 in 2007 to the Camden City Curfew Program. Likewise, 5 years after its inception, Denver had recorded a 26 percent decrease in juvenile victims of crime and a 50 percent decrease in juvenile suspect rates (juveniles accused of or alleged to have committed a crime).

Several studies also indicate that curfews may make an impact on juvenile trauma rates. [Researcher Steven J.] Weiss and colleagues examined pediatric emergency medical services (or EMS) transports before and after the implementation of a New Orleans city curfew. They found that there was a significant decrease in pediatric transports and in pediatric trauma transports. [Researchers David V.] Shatz, [Chi] Zhang, and [Mark] McGrath found that the curfew law implemented in Dade County, Fla., led to a significant decrease in pediatric trauma volume at the county's level-1 trauma center during curfew hours, while rates remained stable during noncurfew hours. In a comparison of cities with curfews and cities without curfews, [researchers David F.] Preusser, [Paul L.] Zador, and [Allan F.] Williams found that curfews were associated with a 23 percent reduction in fatal injury for 13- to 17-year-olds for the period of 9:00 p.m. to 5:59 a.m.

| "There is little empirical evidence that curfews deter crime and reduce juvenile victimization."

Curfews Do Not Reduce Crime and Protect Urban Youth

Tony Favro

In the following viewpoint, Tony Favro questions the effectiveness and legality of curfews. Curfews, the author maintains, suffer from a lack of reliable research and have been challenged in courts for infringing parental and individual civil rights. Instead of a solution to juvenile crime, curfews are best used as a tool to connect troubled children and adolescents to counseling, youth programs, and mentoring, he concludes. Favro is a consultant for urban planning and editor of the website City Mayors, an international think tank for urban affairs.

As you read, consider the following questions:

1. What complex social problems does curfew legislation try to solve, in the author's opinion?

Tony Favro, "Youth Curfews Popular with American Cities but Effectiveness and Legality Are Questioned," City Mayors, July 21, 2009. www.citymayors.com. Reproduced by permission of City Mayors.

2. What methodological problems complicate the study of curfews and crime rates, in Favro's view?

3. What constitutional arguments do opponents of curfews offer, as stated by the author?

At least 500 US cities have curfews on teenage youth, including 78 of the 92 cities with a population greater than 180,000. In most of these cities, curfews prohibit children under 18 from being on the streets after 11:00 pm during the week and after midnight on weekends. About 100 cities also have daytime curfews to keep children off the streets during school hours. The curfews are designed to prevent crime, increase parental responsibility for their children, and give police greater ability to stop people involved in suspicious activity.

Youth curfews are popular with the public because they are inexpensive relative to other crime-fighting tools and have an easy-to-understand logic: If kids are home, they won't commit crimes or be victims of crimes. However, there is little empirical evidence that curfews deter crime and reduce juvenile victimization. Curfews are also challenged on constitutional grounds.

History of Youth Curfews

The first youth curfew was adopted by Omaha, Nebraska, in 1880. In 1884, President Benjamin Harrison called curfews "the most important municipal regulation for the protection of children in American homes from the vices of the street."

Chicago, the nation's largest city with a curfew, passed its law in 1955. By 1960, 60 of the 110 US cities with a population over 100,000 had curfews. Thirty years later, 200 US cities had a population over 100,000, and 150 of these cities had curfews. In 1996, President Bill Clinton endorsed youth curfews for helping "keep our children out of harm's way." In the late-1990s, the US Conference of Mayors and the National League of Cities began issuing Best Practices for cities to follow when enacting curfews.

In 2000, when 337 cities had curfews, Bob Knight, then-President of the National League of Cities and mayor of Wichita, Kansas, called curfews "a growing trend in the United States as city officials look for answers to ensure the safety of youth in their communities." Since 2000, the number of US cities with curfews increased an estimated 50 per cent to about 500.

Effectiveness of Youth Curfews

In the earliest years, curfews were aimed almost exclusively at keeping young criminals off the street. Today, new curfew legislation often tries to solve more complex social ills, such as the inability of parents to control their children and the alarming number of innocent children who are the unintended victims of drive-by shootings and other adult violence.

Three years after San Antonio, Texas, enacted a curfew, the victimization of youth dropped 84 per cent. Detroit, Cincinnati, New Orleans, and other cities report similar results. Still, the precise reasons for the decrease in crime rates are difficult to discern. There are many factors—weather, for example—that must be considered. "Despite their popularity with local governments, little is known about the effects of curfew laws on youth outcomes," according to a study of the impact of juvenile curfew laws by Patrick Kline of the University of Michigan.

There are several methodological problems which make an empirical study of curfews difficult. Cities enact their curfews in different years; some in response to an outbreak of youth violence, others as a measure to prevent youth violence. This complicates the comparison of before-and-after crime rates between cities. Curfews also appear to affect youth above the curfew age, who look younger and are thus often stopped by police. Juvenile arrests increase significantly in most cities with

Not a Panacea

One study conducted by Mike Males and Dan Macallair, which focused on curfew laws in California, found that youth curfews do not reduce youth crime and if anything may actually increase delinquent activities. For the entire state of California there was no category of crime (misdemeanors, violent crime, property crime, etc.) that significantly declined in association with youth curfews. In a comprehensive systematic review of the existing literature on curfews, criminologist Ken Adams found little evidence that juvenile crime and victimization were influenced in any way by the implementation of curfew laws.

These results indicate that juvenile curfews are not the panacea some people believe. It is possible that after curfews are implemented, victimization levels increase significantly during non-curfew hours, an indication that rather than suppressing delinquency, curfews merely shift the time of occurrence of the offenses.

Larry V. Siegel and Brandon C. Welsh,
Juvenile Delinquency: Theory, Practice, and Law, *2008.*

curfews, and the long-term impact of this criminalization of youth is unknown. For these and other reasons, according to Kline, "it's not surprising that past studies have typically failed to find an effect of curfews on juvenile crime."

The Courts

In addition to citing the lack of definitive research that curfews reduce crime by youth, opponents also maintain that curfews prevent parents from exercising full control over their children and allow children to be unreasonably detained. Curfews, according to opponents, are a violation of an individual's constitutional rights to freedom of movement, freedom of expression and association, and equal protection under the law, as well as the due process right to raise one's children without undue interference from the government.

Several urban curfew laws have been tested in court. In 1991, the American Civil Liberties Union (ACLU) challenged Dallas, Texas' curfew law. The US Supreme Court let the Dallas law stand on the grounds that it allows several exceptions for an underage person to break the curfew, such as coming home from work or carrying a note from their parents. Many cities now use the Dallas statute as a model for their curfew laws.

Still, the ACLU and others have been successful in striking down curfews in a number of cities. Rochester, New York, provides a good example. Rochester enacted a night-time curfew in 2007. In 2009, the New York Court of Appeals deemed it unconstitutional.

After finding that the curfew unconstitutionally infringes upon the free speech rights of youth, the judges wrote in their decision, "We also conclude that the curfew imposes an unconstitutional burden on a parent's substantive due process rights. The city asserts that the ordinance promotes 'parental supervision' of minors . . . But the curfew fails to offer parents enough flexibility or autonomy in supervising their children."

The judges also wrote, "Further, we conclude that the crime statistics produced by the defendants do not support the objectives of Rochester's nocturnal curfew. Although the statistics show that minors are suspects and victims in roughly 10 per cent of violent crimes committed between curfew hours . . . what they really highlight is that minors are far more likely to commit or be victims of crime outside curfew hours and that it is adults, rather than the minors, who commit and are victims of the vast majority of violent crime—83.6 per cent and 87.8 percent respectively—during curfew hours."

Rochester Mayor Robert Duffy reacted harshly to the court's ruling: "Unfortunately, this decision takes away our capacity to use the curfew as a common sense public safety tool." The New York Civil Liberties Union responded by saying, "Improving public safety is a laudable goal. And there are ways to accomplish it that don't involve infringing on the Constitution."

Successful Crime Prevention

While the effectiveness and constitutionality of curfews will continue to be studied and debated in universities, courts, and City Halls, what seems clear is that, at best, a curfew is a tool to identify a problem, not a solution.

Cities with the most effective curfews, such as Minneapolis, Minnesota, do not deliver merely punitive consequences to children, but connect them to counseling, social, and recreational programs. They offer mentoring and positive adult role models and leadership in schools and neighborhoods. They establish good communications between police, parents, schools, social agencies, and youth. Curfews, in other words, are one part of a comprehensive safety net for children and families.

As Minneapolis Mayor R.T. Rybek explains, "We are all responsible for the kids in our community."

> *"Every aspect of the [charter] school is designed to steer students away from stumbling blocks and onto success."*

Charter Schools Can Benefit Urban Students

Monica Rohr

Monica Rohr is a writer for the Associated Press. In the following viewpoint, she asserts that YES Prep North Central, a charter school in Houston, Texas, is designed to send underprivileged, inner-city youths to college. The charter school successfully creates a campus culture of discipline and achievement, Rohr claims, with high expectations and a support network of faculty and staff. As a result, each student is determined to gain admission to his or her chosen university and fulfill YES Prep's aim of securing college enrollment for all of its graduates, the author maintains.

As you read, consider the following questions:

1. How does Rohr describe the student body at YES Prep?

2. In the author's words, how does YES Prep help students succeed?

Monica Rohr, "Can Inner-City Charter Schools Succeed? Students Say 'YES,'" *USA Today*, January 4, 2010. Reproduced by permission.

3. How do seminars prepare juniors and seniors for college enrollment, according to Rohr?

It was Deadline Day at YES Prep North Central, the day college applications were supposed to be finished, the day essays, personal statements and a seemingly endless series of forms needed to be slipped into white envelopes, ready for submission.

The day the school's first graduating class would take one leap closer to college.

The seniors inside Room A121 were sprinting, scurrying and stumbling to the finish line. They hunched over plastic banquet tables, brows furrowed and eyed fixed on the screens of Dell laptop computers. Keyboards clattered, papers rustled and sighs swept across the room like waves of nervous energy.

So much was riding on this.

The reputation of a charter school built around the mission of sending every student to college. The hopes of parents who wanted more for their children than they had attained. The expectations of younger siblings, schoolmates and friends hungry for role models.

And above all, the dreams of 43 North Central seniors determined to turn stereotypes and statistics upside-down.

But first, those applications had to sparkle.

"We need that stuff ASAP," said Chad Spurgeon, sounding more like a coach before a big game than North Central's director of college counseling. In a baggy blue Creighton University sweat shirt, Spurgeon looked the part, too. "You've got to make sure these are where they need to be."

Around the room, jangled nerves seemed to jangle just a little more.

Eric Salazar, a soft-spoken student at the top of the senior class, gnawed absently on his cuticles.

Brandon Gunter, normally jovial, rummaged frantically through his backpack. "I'm getting the feeling I forgot my essay at home. This. Is. Not. Happening," Brandon fretted, his voice inching higher with each word.

Fernando Luna hunkered in the back of the room, staring at his computer screen and thinking of everything he still needed to finish. The solidly built teenager with deep dimples smiled serenely, but inside, he could feel the pressure. With this application, college, long a dream, was suddenly, tantalizingly, nerve-rackingly within grasp.

He muttered, as if to reassure himself: "This is just an essay. I can tackle it. I can do it."

A Vague Notion

A few years earlier, college had been a vague notion for most of these students. It was a name emblazoned on a sweat shirt, an ivy-covered campus on a movie screen, a pathway for people more privileged or prepared.

"I didn't know anything about college," said Carol Cabrera, 17, the oldest child of a construction worker father and a stay-at-home mom, Mexican immigrants who had not made it past high school.

Elizabeth Martinez and Brandon Gunter, both 17, had long been told that a college education paved the road to a better life. But they didn't know how to turn the ambition into reality.

In middle school, Eric Salazar often felt like the only student turning in homework, the only one striving for higher standards. Even his teachers expected little from the students.

Fernando Luna saw his future limited to technical schools or vocational colleges.

"It's more difficult to be successful if you're ashamed to be the only person on time for a test, the only one doing homework," said Fernando, 17, as the five North Central seniors sat at a table in the school's cafeteria in early September. "College was a goal for me, but not a tangible possibility."

Then these five students stepped inside North Central, where college for all is not just a catch phrase. It's a vision infused into the fabric of the YES Prep charter school system.

YES Prep—the name is an acronym for Youth Engaged in Service—was founded 11 years ago by Chris Barbic, a Teacher for America alumnus who shaped his vision around a simple, singular goal: Every student is expected to go to a four-year college, succeed there and return to give back to their community.

It was an ambitious goal for a population often underserved or expected to fail.

More than 90% of YES Prep students are first-generation college-bound; 80% come from low-income families and 96% are Hispanic or African-American. Most students enter the charter school at least one grade level behind in math and English.

Almost every student can name friends or relatives who have succumbed to the streets, dropping out of school, landing in jail or getting entangled with gangs.

The Culture-of-College Formula

At YES Prep, every aspect of the school is designed to steer students away from stumbling blocks and onto success. Longer school days. A strict discipline code. A challenging curriculum. A small teacher-student ratio.

There is also a nonstop conversation about college. Middle school homerooms are named after the teacher's alma mater. On Fridays, everyone is encouraged to wear shirts with college logos. Banners, posters and signs in hallways and classrooms tout schools.

A popular bumper sticker sums up the school's mission: "Will my child go to college? The answer is YES."

Parents of students must sign a contract agreeing to commit to the YES Prep philosophy and rules. Many parents turned to YES after becoming frustrated with the quality of public schools in their neighborhoods. Students are admitted through a lottery, with almost 4,000 now on a waiting list to enter.

So far, the culture-of-college formula seems to be working. At YES Prep Southeast, the only campus to serve 12th graders until this year [2009–2010], 100% of seniors have been accepted to college since the first class graduated in 2001—matriculating at some 266 schools, including Harvard, Yale and other Ivy League universities.

This year, North Central, which opened in 2003 and serves 6th through 12th grade, will become the second YES Prep campus to graduate seniors—and the class of 2010 doesn't want to be the first to tarnish the charter school's record.

"We are the leaders here," said Carol, a petite girl with a pixie's grin. "We have to set the record for everyone else to follow."

On most days, Room A121 is home to Junior and Senior Seminar.

In 11th grade, the school's two college counselors, Spurgeon and Merrily Brannigan, steer students through an introduction to the college application process and an intensive preparation for the SAT. In 12th grade, students focus on completing applications, refining essays and resumes, visiting colleges and applying for scholarships and financial aid.

The seminar courses also give the counselors substantial time to work with individual students, something not feasible in larger urban districts. At her previous job in a large Houston school district, Brannigan had a caseload of 500 students and dealt with issues ranging from teen pregnancy to suicide attempts in addition to college counseling.

Ownership of the Process

At YES Prep, Brannigan and Spurgeon focus almost entirely on college counseling for 43 seniors and 60 juniors.

"We learn a lot about the kids, and they learn a lot about themselves," said Spurgeon. "It's no secret that there's only so much we can do. They have to take ownership of the process."

By mid-November, most of the Class of 2010 had done just that.

Carol Cabrera set aside her weekends to fill out applications and work on her essays. Inside the modest brick house built by her father, her desk was piled with college pamphlets and brochures. Her latest report cards were tucked under the clear plastic tablecloth on her family's kitchen table—a constant reminder of how far she has come.

Elizabeth Martinez was spending her lunch hours chipping away at her applications in the school's still-developing library—a few bookshelves and a collection of mismatched sofas and chairs in the former entrance to a church that once housed North Central. The school grew around the church but still uses the old sanctuary as an auditorium.

But on Nov. 20, the day the school set as application deadline day, many seniors were still scrambling to finish applications for the University of Texas and Texas A&M University, the schools with the most pressing deadlines.

In Senior Seminar, the 50-minute class period seemed to rocket by.

Suddenly, an anguished moan froze the entire room.

"Oh-oh!"

"I don't like that face," Spurgeon said, catching sight of Sally Arias' stricken expression.

"I deleted it. How did I do this? I deleted my essay," Arias whispered. "I think I'm gonna cry."

Mayra Valle rushed to her side. "We'll find it. We have to. This is your future."

A few feet away, Eric Salazar covered his face with both hands. He was nearly finished with applications for Texas A&M, Cornell and Duke, his top choices. A few days earlier, a

Cornell recruiter had even called to make sure he would be applying, a very promising sign.

"It gave me a tremendous sense of accomplishment," said Salazar, an aspiring engineer who wore a maroon Texas A&M T-shirt. "Going up to your senior year, you don't get it yet. You just work hard because teachers tell you to do it and you have to trust it will pay off."

Yet, he could not afford to slack off. An essay for Cornell still needed honing. Eric was writing about a person who had inspired him. The first line: "My dad is a carpenter."

In the back corner, Brandon had finally fished out his errant essay. Now, he was typing answers to an A&M financial aid questionnaire. "My mom is a single parent. She's struggling to raise my sister and me," wrote Brandon, who hopes to study engineering at Dartmouth.

Fernando Luna looked over Brandon's shoulder then turned back to his own computer screen with a sigh. Texas A&M was one of his dream schools, and he was still far behind on his application.

Spurgeon picked up on the sigh.

"How's your essay coming?" he asked, bending by Fernando's side. "Is it gonna be ready?"

"Ummm," wavered Fernando, who wants to be a petroleum engineer. "It's gonna be a long night."

It would have to be. Senior Seminar was over.

Time for next period.

The path to senior year has been strewn with obstacles and "aha" moments.

Sticking It Out

The class of 2010, which started with about 100 students in 6th grade, has been whittled to 43. YES Prep loses about 5% of its population each year, as students move, transfer to other schools or drop out.

Using Resources More Wisely

Democracy Prep, like other city charters, spends about as much per pupil as the surrounding district public schools do: though it doesn't receive capital funds from the state, it makes up the difference in philanthropic contributions and by locating the sixth grade in a public school virtually rent-free. But the school's charter status allows it to use its resources more wisely than the district schools do. Democracy Prep saves money by employing many young teachers, substituting 401(k)-style plans for the gold-plated, defined-benefit pensions bestowed in the traditional public sector, and eliminating administrative bloat. Thanks to these savings, the school can pay its teachers 10 percent above the traditional public school pay scale. The school also has money left over to provide students with enriching activities: before they graduate, Democracy Prep's kids, many of whom had rarely ventured out of their neighborhood, will have visited more than 75 college campuses and set foot on five continents. Again, all of this is done for about the same amount of money that advocates for traditional public schools say is insufficient to purchase even basic resources.

Marcus A. Winters, City Journal, *Summer 2010.*

Those who stick it out must confront resistance from old friends, the temptation to slack off, worries about college costs.

"My cousins would say, 'You are such a loser. You have to go to school on Saturdays,'" recalled Carol Cabrera. "Now I say: 'I'm going to college and you're not.'"

At first, Carol chafed at the increased academic demands and strict discipline at North Central and often begged her parents to take her out. Then, she started picturing herself at college, going on to a career in broadcast journalism, achieving what her parents had not.

"We know that a lot of things outside school that have little to do with academics will affect academics," said North Central school director Mark DiBella. "So we try to create a support system at this school. When they go back into their neighborhoods, they can hearken back to this community of like-minded people."

At North Central, students and faculty alike refer to the school as a family and speak of a special commitment. At weekly "family gatherings," all the students in each class assemble to give "shoutouts" to classmates or teachers who they think deserve praise. YES Prep also helps every student find funding for college.

The school is awash with inspirational sayings—on bulletin boards, newsletters and bright orange signs on the awning over outside walkways: "The strong should take care of the weak." "Anything worth doing is worth doing right." "We are here to make a difference." "We always leave a place better than we found it." "When we all pull together we move mountains."

Students sometimes repeat them without realizing it.

"By the 12th grade, these messages are just a part of you," said Brandon Gunter. "Everyone's on the same page here. It's like physics, like Newton's law. Something stays in motion unless something negative stops it. Here, there is nothing negative to stop us."

The Turning Point

For many students, the turning point comes during the school's spring and summer trips, when they tour college campuses and participate in camping and community service trips. It's often their first time away from home and the first time actually visiting a college campus. The experience can be transformational.

"If it hadn't been for the trips, I wouldn't know how it feels to be away from home ...," said Carol Cabrera. "Now, I've been out there, away from my parents. It makes it harder for me to think about staying in Houston for school."

For Fernando Luna, the "aha" moment came much closer to home.

Fernando was working a summer job at a farmers market when he noticed that people seemed to be looking through him. All they saw was another manual laborer, he thought. No one could see his aspirations or his intellect.

"If I don't get an education," he remembers thinking, "I'll be letting all the people who support me down and I'll be proving the people who don't believe in me right."

Carol Cabrera wrinkled her forehead in exasperation.

With only 20 minutes left in her Senior Seminar class, Carol was surrounded by white envelopes and application packages. She had already submitted 13 applications, including one to her top choice, Whittier College in California.

Now, on deadline day, she was having second thoughts.

"I feel like I'm applying to schools I might not get into. I need to get into more solid schools," said Carol. "I'm frustrated in the sense that I don't know what's going to happen."

Glancing at the list of schools on her computer screen, then at the scattered applications, she exhaled deeply.

"I'm tired. I want to go home, take a shower and go to sleep. As a whole senior class, we're tired."

On the other side of the room, Elizabeth Martinez was fending off her own butterflies.

She fingered her application to an Alabama college, her safety school, that was the last application she needed to mail. She'd worried it might get lost in the pile of applications the counselors needed to send out, but now the essays were polished, the questionnaires completed.

She had already finished the paperwork for her other schools, including first-choice Vanderbilt University in Nashville.

But meeting deadlines wasn't her only worry. Just a month earlier at a parent-student conference, Elizabeth had cried as she talked about moving away from Houston. Now, she said, "I'm sure everything's going to be OK. I hope so."

She stiffened her shoulders, sealed the envelope and placed the Alabama application on the pile.

Now, the very last step: Plopping in front of her laptop, she clicked the online application. And in no time, a mouse click brought a slow, shy smile to the anxious teenager's face.

"Congratulations, Elizabeth!" the on-screen message flashed, "You have successfully submitted your application."

"Charter schools . . . do not enroll the very troubled, high-need, at-risk students who pose the greatest challenge to public education."

Charter Schools Do Not Benefit Needy Urban Students

Sharon Higgins and Caroline Grannan

Sharon Higgins is a blogger and parent of students in public school in Oakland, California. Caroline Grannan is the education writer at the San Francisco Examiner *and a former editor at the* San Jose Mercury News. *In the following viewpoint, Higgins and Grannan claim that charter schools leave out urban students who are most in need or most at risk. According to the authors, admission to charter schools is by request—troubled parents of youths are unlikely to make such efforts. Higgins and Grannan also contend that unlike public school districts, charter schools are not responsible for "undesirable" students and can turn them away, and, as a result, dramatically underserve those with special needs.*

Sharon Higgins and Caroline Grannan, "Charters Exclude the Most Challenging Students, Parts 1 and 2," Change.org, March 17, 2009. Reproduced by permission of the authors.

As you read, consider the following questions:

1. How does the performance of charter schools compare to that of public schools, in Higgins and Grannan's view?

2. How do the authors respond to the claim that charter schools select students through a lottery when applicants outnumber seats, according to the authors?

3. What makes up the enrollment process to San Francisco's best charter school, as described by Higgins and Grannan?

President [Barack] Obama admires charter schools and has called for opening more in the United States. Though we trust that he has students' best interests at heart, we also believe he is badly misinformed.

Charter schools get overwhelmingly positive press and make a lot of claims about their success. But actually, numerous studies confirm that their achievement is indistinguishable from that of traditional public schools. Some are very successful, some are troubled and struggling, and the rest are somewhere in between—just like traditional public schools.

One of the boasts by their proponents is that charter schools enroll "the poorest of the poor." But is that accurate? We're urban public school parents (Caroline is in San Francisco and Sharon is in Oakland, Calif.) who see the insides of schools in our day-to-day lives, and we recognize why that claim is misleading.

The truth is that charter schools may enroll some very low-income students, but they do not enroll the very troubled, high-need, at-risk students who pose the greatest challenge to public education. (There are some specialty charter schools specifically for juvenile offenders or other defined groups; we are not referring to that type but to general education charter schools.)

Enrollment at all charter schools is, by law, entirely by request. No student is assigned to a charter school by default. That means "self-selection" occurs at all of them, inherently, by definition.

Parents Who Care, Parents Who Do Not

That is, parents who care about their kids' education enough to make the effort to learn about and request a school are the ones whose kids attend charter schools. Parents who don't have it together to pay attention, care, or take action to try to improve their kids' education do not choose charter schools. Thus their kids—obviously likely to be the most challenged and challenging—are left in the traditional public schools.

Parent #1: Even though she is low-income, she has a relatively stable income. She also has extended family and/or community support. She is lucky because she happens to not be prone to substance abuse or mental illness. Even though she has always been poor, she has had the good fortune to acquire enough information and inspiration in life to permit her to adopt parenting values more aligned with America's middle-class. This results in her regularly, and consciously, making her very best efforts at raising her children with an educationally minded approach.

Parent #2: She is also low-income, but her week-to-week existence is very unstable, some years worse than others. She is highly stressed and perhaps has a degree of untreated mental illness (likely mild to severe depression, or post-traumatic stress disorder). She also has substance abuse problems, ranging from either mild or severe. Her family and/or community support is weak, or abusive, and her parenting takes second place to moment-to-moment survival. Her life has been highly socioeconomically restricted, so she has never known anyone who could have modeled any different parenting style for her. In terms of her children, she is not very educationally minded, because she has never learned what that approach is all about.

Which parent is more likely to seek a charter school? Which parent will be more likely to "appropriately" respond to teachers and report card results? Which parent will be more likely to turn off the TV and remind her kids that homework needs to get done? Which parent will still be sleeping at 8 am, leaving it up to her children to get to school on time, if at all. Which parent will be moving from apartment to apartment with her children in tow, year after year?

The husband of one of the authors of this [viewpoint] works with the indigent people living in Alameda County, California, who have been charged with crimes. Every day he deals with parents who have been charged with drug possession, prostitution, and other crimes. These are the types of parents who aren't likely to be researching the best charter schools for their children, and filling out all the forms. These types of parents are not the majority in Oakland, but they are quite numerous nonetheless. Their children are enrolled in Oakland's traditional public schools.

This is what charter school self-selection is all about.

A "Blind Lottery"

Charter advocates' usual response to this explanation is to deny that there is such a thing as families that are less motivated and stable. They claim that "all parents care enough." All we can say is that those people need to get out more.

And what about the question of whether charter schools actively pick and choose their students? Charter schools are supposed to admit everyone and choose by lottery if they have more applications than seats. However, does anyone believe that there are regulators somehow watching over the entire enrollment process, from receipt of the applications to the implementation of a lottery, if any?

If a charter school chooses to conduct itself this way, it is free as a bird to "not have space" for applicants who appear undesirable for whatever reason. It's amply documented that

Charter Schools and Segregation

Charter schools attract a higher percentage of black students than traditional public schools, in part because they tend to be located in urban areas. As a result, charter school enrollment patterns display high levels of minority segregation, trends that are particularly severe for black students.

While segregation for blacks among all public schools has been increasing for nearly two decades, black students in charter schools are far more likely than their traditional public school counterparts to be educated in intensely segregated settings. At the national level, seventy percent of black charter school students attend intensely segregated minority charter schools (which enroll 90–100% of students from under-represented minority backgrounds), or *twice* as many as the share of intensely segregated black students in traditional public schools. Some charter schools enrolled populations where 99% of the students were from under-represented minority backgrounds. Forty-three percent of black charter school students attended these extremely segregated minority schools, a percentage which was, by far, the highest of any other racial group, and nearly *three times* as high as black students in traditional public schools.

Erica Frankenberg, Genevieve Siegel-Hawley, and Jia Wang,
Choice Without Equity: Charter School Segregation
and the Need for Civil Rights Standards, *January 2010.*

charter schools all over the country, overall, dramatically underserve special education students, for example.

Charter advocates will counter that traditional public schools can manage to not enroll or to "counsel out" a challenging student too. Sure, but that student is still the responsibility of the public school district, and will land in another school run by a colleague of the administrator who managed to deny/remove the student. If a charter school contrives to not enroll or get rid of a challenging student, it never has to set eyes on or give a thought to that student again.

San Francisco's most successful charter school, a high school, requires a 9-page enrollment application—including transcripts; teacher recommendations; an essay; and signed commitments to behavior, academic effort, volunteering and so forth by the student and parent. Then the administrators claim to put all the applicants in a "blind lottery." It strikes us as exceptionally naive to believe those applicants aren't being screened.

But even parents who give the school the benefit of the doubt in trusting that it runs a "blind lottery" agree that the application process serves to weed out those who are not highly motivated.

An interesting book, "Hard Lessons" by Jonathan Schorr, a former journalist who has since gone to work in the charter-school world, follows the founding and first year of an Oakland, Calif., charter school, the Ernestine C. Reems Academy of Technology and Arts. The book is pro-charter in tone, but it still portrays the school deliberately rejecting special-education students.

And yet, despite the advantages of serving a student population that is predisposed to be higher-functioning, charter schools overall do not show higher achievement than traditional public schools. So why do they win such acclaim, including from the Oval Office? It's a mystery.

> *"Many [mentoring] clubs [are] cropping up in public schools across the city to help at-risk youngsters succeed in schools and their communities."*

Mentoring Programs Help Urban Youth

Leslie Talmadge

In the following viewpoint, Leslie Talmadge writes that mentoring clubs impact the lives of at-risk inner-city youths through guidance and support. The author asserts that several programs in Boston schools provide vulnerable adolescent boys a safe space and role models to follow. Using sports, field trips, and open discussions, the mentoring groups teach constructive behaviors, morals, and the value of education, Talmadge says. The author's writings have appeared in the Christian Science Monitor *and* Boston Globe.

As you read, consider the following questions:

1. In Ingrid Carney's opinion, as cited by Talmadge, who are the most vulnerable students?

2. What issues are discussed at Live Brothers, as stated by the author?

Leslie Talmadge, "For the Boys in the 'Hood," *Boston Globe*, March 9, 2008. Reproduced by permission of the author.

3. What is the goal of the peer-mentoring program at East Boston High School, as stated by Talmadge?

About 30 boys sat quietly in a circle at the Henry Dearborn Middle School in Roxbury, their hands clasped in their laps, their heads lowered.

Arthur Collins greeted the boys, most of Cape Verdean ancestry, and instructed them on how to slow down their breathing and start thinking about how they're feeling. Then he praised them for not getting into trouble.

"Not many people were sent down to the office. I appreciate that," said Collins, a Dorchester native who is a manager in the Boston Public Schools. Then he tells the boys to raise their heads, pair off, and "give dap," a form of greeting that's part handshake, part high-five.

The boys are "angry with each other and with life," Collins said before the session. By coming to the Dearborn's Live (Loyal, Intelligent, Victorious, Everlasting) Brothers program, "they can talk about their anger and frustration," he said. "It doesn't fix it, but it gives them a way to cope with it."

Live Brothers is one of the many all-boys clubs cropping up in public schools across the city to help at-risk youngsters succeed in schools and their communities.

"If you look at who is dying in the streets . . . and if you look at the achievement gap, the most vulnerable students, the most underperforming students, are boys of color," said Ingrid Carney, a deputy superintendent with the Boston Public Schools.

That's why Carney started the "10 Boys" initiative last year [in 2007], a program designed to help black and Latino boys improve their MCAS [Massachusetts Comprehensive Assessment System] scores. Today, there are about 85 10 Boys clubs, which are run by school administrators, as well as other all-boys groups, such as Live Brothers.

Clearly, students are in need of emotional support along with academic support, Carney said, and they need to develop leadership skills. So, if schools can figure out how to help the students at greatest risk, "we will know how to help every child," she said, adding that such programs may be "saving lives."

"People outside the neighborhood have no idea the level of dysfunction, trauma these guys are dealing with," said Byron Beaman, a special-education specialist who runs all-boys programs for middle schools in Dorchester, East Boston, and other parts of the city.

Likening his students to soldiers who have to be constantly vigilant because "everybody is a potential threat," Beaman said creating a safe space is vital.

At the Dearborn, Live Brothers meets every day. (Ten of the roughly 35 members also participate in the school's 10 Boys club, run by the headmaster.) There is no set curriculum. Lessons include how to shake hands properly to how to dress professionally (don't "sag" your pants).

The boys also delve into weighty topics—sex, drugs, race, principles, morality. Nothing's taboo.

Relationships are at the heart of these clubs. The boys talk about the friends they've made, and their respect for Collins and "Big Mike," as they call Mike McDonald, who is a life-success coach for the Boston Urban Youth Foundation and helps Collins run Live Brothers.

McDonald does things a father or brother might do, such as watch the boys' football games, take them to church, and play basketball with them. In a pinch, he even loans them money.

"Anytime you see me, you're going to see my kids," said McDonald, who grew up in Harlem. "Boys their age get into mischief, and in the inner city, mischief can equal violence."

"Mr. McDonald, he's like my pops. He's the only role model in my life," said Antonio Stroud, 14.

Effectiveness of Mentoring

Evidence for the effectiveness of mentoring was provided by an impact study of Big Brothers/Big Sisters. Control youth were placed on a waiting list for 18 months and the experimental group youth were matched with mentors. The 2 groups were compared on a number of outcomes. Relative to control youth, matched participants reported skipping fewer days of school, lower levels of substance initiation and use, less physical aggression, higher scholastic competence, attendance, and grades. In addition to these behavioral and academic outcomes, mentoring relationships were associated with improvements in the youth's relationships with their parents and peers.

Regina Day Langhout, Jean E. Rhodes, and Lori N. Osborne,
Journal of Youth and Adolescence, *August 4, 2004.*

Across the city at East Boston High School, Adrian Husbands, a 15-year-old with braids, braces, and a shy smile, said, "I thought school was just a joke."

Before joining the school's all-boys, peer-mentoring program, which pairs at-risk freshmen with successful juniors, Husbands said he never listened to teachers or did his work. "I wasn't really caring," he said. But he realized that he wants "to be smart. I don't want to be a loser."

His grades and his attitude have improved.

"I'm starting to get some respect from people around here," said Husbands, who wants to become a firefighter.

"And I'm enjoying it."

Rich LaCara, a history teacher at the high school and coordinator of East Boston's Male (Mentoring, Achievement, Leadership, Excellence) program, said he was drawn to it because "I see these kids who are smart who keep on failing for stupid reasons. . . . One different move and they could've been on the right path."

Kevin Giberti, who teaches math and helps with the program, said one of his students skipped the algebra final to go to the beach. He flunked the class and had to repeat it.

These kinds of clubs are important, he said, because "this group stresses what's right, what's wrong" and teaches students to set goals.

Ultimately, the goal is to help students graduate from high school and, ideally, go to college, said Michael Smith, one of the deans who helped start the peer-mentoring program.

On a recent "Dress for Success" day, about 10 of the older boys wore shirts and ties that Smith bought for them at Sears the day after Christmas. Discussing Sean Covey's book, "The 7 Habits of Highly Effective Teens," the boys wrestled with what it means to be proactive rather than reactive, and they reflected on their bad habits, such as procrastination.

Every other week, the boys play sports. They also take field trips. On a recent trip to Boston University, for example, students toured the campus, spoke with members of the men's swim team, and watched a basketball game.

At the Dearborn school, Live Brothers has helped keep the students "focused and quiet," principal Carroll Blake said.

Without the program, Stroud said, "I'd probably be failing or getting into trouble on the street.

"It's motivating me to be a better man."

| "*Despite the popularity of mentoring, research suggests that many current programs may be failing youth.*"

Not All Mentoring Programs Are Effective

Society for Research in Child Development

In the following viewpoint, the Society for Research in Child Development (SRCD) advises that many youth-mentoring programs are ineffective. Although research indicates that young people who participate in high-quality mentorships are more likely to graduate from high school, attend college, and avoid gangs, SRCD maintains that some programs do not adhere to proven practices and suffer from high rates of turnover among volunteers, which hinders strong mentoring relationships and drains resources. SRCD is a nonprofit professional association based in Ann Arbor, Michigan.

As you read, consider the following questions:

1. How are mentoring programs growing, according to SRCD?

2. What features must be present for a mentoring program to be effective, in the author's view?

3. Why is the financial benefit of mentoring programs disappointing, as stated by SRCD?

Three million young people participate in formal one-to-one mentoring relationships in the United States today, six times the number who took part in such programs a decade ago. National interest in mentoring also has risen, as has federal, state, and private funding for these programs. Young people who take part in high-quality mentoring programs are more likely to finish high school, attend college, improve their self-esteem, and stay away from gangs, research has shown. But despite widespread support for mentoring and studies that show what works, most programs fail to incorporate the very features that have been found to make them work, putting youth at risk.

Policy Implications

- Federal funding for mentoring programs has increased substantially over the past decade, with annual Congressional appropriations of $100 million since 2004. State and private funding have added to the increase in programs.

- Big Brothers Big Sisters currently serves 300,000 young people, up from 100,000 in the mid-1990s; the group aims to reach a million by 2010. The Corporation for National and Community Service has called for three million new matches by 2010. MENTOR/National Mentoring Partnership has set a goal of serving 15 million youth. Mentoring was also a key rationale for the establishment of America's Promise—The Alliance for Youth, chaired by [former US secretary of state] Colin Powell.

- Despite the popularity of mentoring, research suggests that many current programs may be failing youth. Studies have found wide variation in programs' effectiveness. In the rush to replicate, quality is sometimes compromised as new programs stray from practices grounded in research. Studies show that the more closely programs adhere to proven practices, the more likely they are to benefit young people.

- Policymakers instituting new programs should pay close attention to the research. They also should look at programs that emphasize the benefit of assessment by building in evaluations. One such program is the Mentoring Initiative for System Involved Youth, sponsored by the Office of Juvenile Justice and Delinquency Prevention (OJJDP) in the U.S. Department of Justice. This initiative is being launched in four demonstration sites and rigorously evaluated within a research-oriented framework. Several large evaluations of school-based mentoring programs should provide additional useful information.

Research Findings

- In the mid-1990s, Big Brothers Big Sisters of America released an impact study citing benefits to youth participating in its programs in emotional, behavioral, social, academic, and career development areas, though the scale of those benefits was small.

- Subsequent studies of mentoring have been mixed. Research based on the National Longitudinal Study of Adolescents found that teens who took part in mentoring programs starting at age 14 were more likely to finish high school, attend college, or work; had higher self-esteem; were less likely to fight or be a member of a gang; and were healthier than their peers who didn't have such relationships.

- Other studies have not found broad benefits for young people, and evaluations of some programs have shown significant problems with programs' ability to support high-quality relationships, leading to less favorable results.

- Research tells us that certain features need to be present in mentoring relationships in order for them to be effective. Such features include close ties between youth and adults, a regular schedule of contact, and duration of at least a year. When the features that have been found to make mentoring relationships successful are lacking, the relationships may not work and may even do harm. A lack of compatibility, insufficient skills on the part of the mentor, infrequent contact, short duration, and the absence of a close bond can keep mentoring relationships from reaching their potential.

Mentoring Facts at a Glance

- Site-based mentoring, in which young people and mentors meet at school or in the workplace, was a rarity 15 years ago. It now accounts for more than half of mentoring programs, with most taking place in elementary schools.

- Not all mentoring programs are as effective as the originals on which they are based.

- Successful mentoring programs identify the critical elements, assess the "market," and provide ongoing supervision and monitoring. One such program is the Across Ages Mentoring Program, a school- and community-based drug-prevention initiative that pairs 9- to 13-year-olds with adults over 55.

- The results of preliminary studies of cost-benefit ratios for youth mentoring programs are disappointing. Benefits of participation in the Big Brothers Big Sisters program, for example, exceeded costs by only the narrowest of margins (an estimated $1.01 benefit for each $1 of cost) when including both taxpayer and other costs.

• High rates of volunteer turnover are a major drain on mentoring programs. Despite programs' considerable investment in mentor recruitment, matching, training, and supervision, as many as 50 percent of relationships end prematurely. To address these problems, many programs are lowering the bar for volunteers, reducing the time commitment and requiring less frequent meetings. These changes run counter to research showing the benefits of longer, more intensive relationships.

Periodical Bibliography

The following articles have been selected to supplement the diverse views presented in this chapter.

Rochelle Boykin Bey   "Combating Youth Violence," *Human Nature Magazine*, September 17, 2010.

Teresa Ann Boeckel   "Curfews' Mixed Reviews: Some Argue That Daytime Provisions Aren't Necessary Because of Truancy Laws," *McClatchy-Tribune Business News*, April 20, 2008.

Anthony Coleman   "Street Justice: Enforcing Curfew and Kids' Safety," nj.com, July 11, 2009.

David Conrads   "He Teaches Inner-City Kids How to Be Smart About Money," *Christian Science Monitor*, September 20, 2010.

Reggie Dylan   "Restructuring Inner-City Schools for the Global Marketplace: Locke High School and the Green Dot 'Solution,'" *Dissident Voice*, September 27, 2008.

Melanie R. Holmes   "Curfews Work to Keep Youths Out of Harm's Way," *Philadelphia Tribune*, June 27, 2008

Mary Murphy   "The Mentors: Six Months In, We Look at the Progress of the Hollywood Reporter and Big Brothers Big Sisters' Mentor Program," *Hollywood Reporter*, July 19, 2010.

Rebecca Schmidt   "Questioning School Choice: An Urban Teacher's Perspective," *Teacher Magazine*, October 29, 2008.

Michael F. Shaughnessy   "An Interview with Patrick Wolf: Vouchers in DC," *Education News*, June 24, 2010.

Sol Stern   "School Choice Is Not Enough," *City Journal*, Winter 2008.

OPPOSING
VIEWPOINTS®
SERIES

CHAPTER 4

What Is the Future of Urban America?

Chapter Preface

In May 2010, the Brookings Institution's Metropolitan Policy Program published "The State of Metropolitan America," a report that attempts to identify the demographic and social trends in America's major cities. In the report's section on race and ethnicity, demographer and sociologist William H. Frey asserts that the fleeing of whites from urban to suburban areas, known as "white flight," has reversed for the first time since it began after World War II. "While whites reside in the suburbs in larger numbers and shares than any minority group, the first decade of the new century brought the United States to a new benchmark population," he states. Frey continues, "For the first time, more than half of all racial and ethnic groups residing in large metro areas live in the suburbs."

Frey examines several shifts in the general population: the majority of Asians and Latinos in metropolitan areas already live in suburbs, and the percentage of African American suburban residents increased from 43 percent in 2000 to 50 percent in 2008. "What some have termed a 'demographic inversion' in metro areas, with whites repopulating cities and minorities moving out to the suburbs, is not yet a widespread phenomenon," says Frey, "but bears watching in the years and decades ahead as metro areas grow even more diverse."

One consequence, speculates urban affairs analyst Aaron M. Renn, is that the "progressive" transit- and smart growth-friendly cities to emerge—such as Portland, Oregon; Austin, Texas; and Seattle, Washington—are also vastly white in population. "This raises troubling questions about these cities," Renn contends. He adds, "Why is it that progressivism in smaller metros is so often associated with low numbers of African Americans? Can you have a progressive city properly so-

called with only a disproportionate handful of African Ameri-
have such relationships.cans in it?"[1] In the following chapter,
the authors debate the future of urban America.

1. Aaron M. Renn, "The White City," *NewGeography*, October 18, 2009, www.newgeogra
phy.com/content/001110-the-white-city.

| "A 'green revolution' is burgeoning in America's cities and towns."

Smart-Growth Policies Will Improve Urban Areas

Neal Peirce

Neal Peirce is a syndicated columnist and chairman of the Cit-istates Group, a network of journalists and civic and business leaders for sustainable urban planning. In the following view-point, Peirce upholds that the smart-growth movement—which emphasizes mass transit and compact, mixed-use land develop-ment—is spreading, to the benefit of America's cities. He claims that improved energy efficiency is now the benchmark of new construction, and that today's green initiatives protect natural environments and curb suburban sprawl and fossil fuel depen-dency. The long-term savings, reduced operating costs, and in-creased property values, Peirce contends, will add momentum to smart growth.

As you read, consider the following questions:

1. What developments make Chicago the "epicenter" of sustainable planning, in Peirce's view?

Neal Peirce, "Sustainable Cities," *American Prospect*, December 17, 2006. Reproduced with permission from The American Prospect, 11 Beacon Street, Suite 1120, Boston, MA 02108.

2. What is the scope of consumption in the United States, as described by the author?

3. How are government zoning codes and regulations changing, in Peirce's view?

A "green revolution" is burgeoning in America's cities and towns.

And it's a surprise. Six years ago, as we exited an economically exuberant but perilously polluting 20th century, the idea would have seemed chimerical [fantastically visionary]. True, by the 1990s we'd begun to talk about community and global sustainability; President [Bill] Clinton even appointed a White House council on the topic. But the conversation proved to be a tad ahead of its time. It exhibited little of the intensity with which the green ideal is today being talked up, and in some places, truly implemented.

A set of mix-and-match developments explain the change. Foremost and scariest among them is the mounting scientific evidence of fast-advancing, potentially cataclysmic global climate change. Then there is the growing realization of oil's short-term future in the dangerous world that September 11 dramatized. Among the results are heightened interest in hybrid cars and renewed focus on wind farms, solar energy, biofuels, and other renewables; a burgeoning "smart-growth" movement in our states and regions; worry on the health front about sedentary lifestyles, obesity, loss of natural connections; green roofs and strong revival of urban parks; and breakthroughs to pinpoint waste and pollution in our great infrastructure systems, enabled by more sophisticated geographic information system (GIS) technology.

If the new, green, urban alchemy has an epicenter, it's Chicago. Once the embodiment of smoky factories and belching locomotives, the erstwhile City of the Big Shoulders has led the new green wave with beds of flowers and blossoming pots hung from new downtown street lamps.

Ten Principles of Smart Growth

1. Make development decisions predictable, fair and cost-effective.
2. Create a range of housing opportunities and choices.
3. Provide a variety of transportation options.
4. Strengthen existing communities and direct development towards them.
5. Preserve natural beauty, parks, farmland and environmentally critical areas.
6. Create complete neighborhoods where daily needs are close at hand.
7. Create a safe, inviting environment for walking.
8. Foster distinctive communities with a strong sense of place.
9. Make efficient use of public investments in infrastructure, schools and services.
10. Put jobs and good schools within reach of all who need them.

TAKEN FROM: David Goldberg, *Choosing Our Community's Future: A Citizen's Guide to Getting the Most Out of New Development*, Washington, D.C.: Smart Growth America, 2005.

A big share of the Chicago credit goes to Mayor Richard J. Daley and his allies. There's a green roof on City Hall and greenery along roadway medians stretching out into the neighborhoods. Asphalt schoolyards have been converted to grass, vacant lots turned into community gardens, greenways and wildlife habitat nurtured. Major reinvestment is occurring in the city's 570 parks, 31 beaches, and 16 historic lagoons. And there's a dramatic "big splash"—3-year-old Millennium Park, $475 million worth of lush greenery, sculpture, fountains, and more on the lakefront that's drawing 4 million visitors a year, many to its stunning outdoor music theater.

Says Chicago Alderman Mary Ann Smith: "We're creating places people want to be, not places people want to flee." In fact, Chicago has registered America's most dramatic "back-to-the-city" movement, with tens of thousands of new downtown residents.

Cities Taking the Lead

But Chicago is no exception. From Philadelphia to Seattle, Boston to San Diego, city officials agree that green urban settings are a critical draw in an era when highly educated, mobile professional workers—the economic gold of the times—gravitate to attractive, welcoming, and healthy places.

What's more, claim the apostles of green, property tax yields from homes and apartments near parks are significantly higher. Tree-lined streets alone increase property values some 15 percent.

Quite quickly in this decade, the familiar definition of "green" has advanced from trees and plants and parks to a much more inclusive vision of city and metropolitan planning. Moreover, it now comprises an array of environmental issues, including energy saving and renewable sources, reduced burning of fossil fuels, cleaner air and water, improved wastewater removal systems, and redevelopment of "brownfields" sites.

Energy standards for buildings—the familiar LEED standards of the U.S. Green Building Council—are a case in point. They're quickly advancing from handfuls of pioneering buildings to a preferred benchmark in new construction. Despite the 2 percent to 4 percent price premium for fully energy-efficient buildings, a growing number of businesses are opting for a LEED standard. Part of the justification is long-term energy savings; another rationale, increasingly cited, is the dramatically increased productivity reported among employees in quality green structures.

Increasing numbers of city governments are moving to the standard that Salt Lake City set recently—requiring LEED approval for any of its own buildings, plus any commercial or residential buildings that receive city funding. "High-performance buildings should be the norm," says Salt Lake City Mayor Rocky Anderson. "Municipal governments have a huge role to play in bringing about that progress."

On the nonprofit side, pioneers in big-scale green building are Enterprise and the Natural Resources Defense Council (NRDC). Their five-year goal, announced in 2004, is 8,500 "environmentally sustainable" and affordable new homes, and a move to make sustainability the mainstream in affordable housing. And not just in construction: The new housing they support must be compact and land efficient, close to transit, and in neighborhoods with ample sidewalks and pathways and shops within walking distance. The idea is that with less auto dependency and easier access to public transportation and jobs, low-income families will have to spend much less on transportation than they now do (on average, 40 cents of every dollar of income at the poverty line). Fewer workers will be forced into long commutes and even more encouraged to walk, with ricochet benefits in saving energy, reducing obesity, and improving overall health.

But what about standard market housing, in typical neighborhoods? Developers nationally are now being asked to "act green" as the U.S. Green Building Council, the NRDC and the Congress for New Urbanism (CNU) create and promote a new LEED-ND ("neighborhood development") standard. "Under this vision," says Chicago architect Doug Farr of the CNU, "both urbanists who pick bad regional sites, and green building practitioners who ignore location and context, will be dancing with dinosaurs."

A Local Response

All these developments link closely to the big climate-change issues of the time. Indeed, global warming has moved quickly up the agenda list of many cities and counties despite—or, arguably, in reaction to—the [George W.] Bush administration's studied indifference. The U.S. Conference of Mayors last June voted to call for sharp reductions in fossil fuel use in all buildings—both for construction as well as heating and cooling. Their stated goal is to make the nation's building stock "carbon-neutral," using no more fuels made from oil, coal or natural gas, by 2030. The stakes are immense: Buildings account for 48 percent of all U.S. energy consumption (well ahead of transportation at 27 percent and industry at 25 percent).

In Seattle, King County Executive Ron Sims is advocating a 2050 mindset. Assume, says Sims, it's already mid-century and one's looking backward to see which of today's major infrastructure and building decisions—for big highways or public transit systems, for example—make sense on the basis of their carbon impact. Meanwhile, Seattle Mayor Greg Nickels issued a "Kyoto Challenge" to the nation's mayors, asking them to pledge they'd meet, in their cities, Kyoto Protocol goals of reducing global warming pollution levels to 7 percent below 1990 levels by 2012. At latest count some 320 mayors—representing 50 million U.S. residents—had signed on.

Seattle and King County initiatives run all the way from partnering with General Motors on development of the country's first and largest hybrid diesel bus fleet to increased portions of biodiesel in vehicle fleets, from the nation's largest hydrogen fuel-cell project (using methane gas from a sewage plant) to efforts to reduce the big carbon footprint of the diesel-burning ships, trains, and trucks that use the city's busy port.

There's also official support for a new "Cascade Agenda," a 100-year conservation and preservation plan for 2.6 million acres of the Puget Sound region's most prized waters, mountains, and communities. The focus is first on channeling growth into denser, well-planned cities, second to save rural lands by a massive new market-based transfer of development rights initiative, and third, with expanded greenery, to create a significant "carbon sink," forests that absorb carbon dioxide emissions.

Back on the East Coast, green revolutionaries in Philadelphia's Office of Watersheds are lead exponents and practitioners of new ways to "daylight" streams turned into culverts. They're working to catch and filter severe storm waters so they don't carry oil and corroding junkyard metals from paved surfaces, not to mention untreated sewage, into rivers and streams. The idea is to adapt city parks, roadways, lawns, and yards with swales and other systems that can absorb and slowly filter water. The vision: to make all of Philadelphia into a kind of great, green sponge that handles its runoff more naturally and assures clean and reliable water for fishing, swimming, and drinking.

Philadelphians have also formed the Schuylkill Action Network (SAN), recognizing they're located downstream from 100 miles of riverside and 2,000 square miles of potentially polluting farms, mines, and factories. Federal and state agencies, plus dozens of upstream communities, belong to SAN—a prime example of how virtually every environmental challenge is regional, and needs to be addressed that way.

Today's roster of green initiatives knows practically no limits. It includes massive tree replanting efforts; conversion of hundreds of miles of once-industrial urban waterfronts to parks and greenways and millions of acres of protected farmlands and forests; concerted efforts to build green schools in which children learn better; and campaigns to expand locally based agriculture and farmers' markets and decrease the pollution from trucks carrying foods over thousands of miles. In Seattle, there's a Hope VI public housing/mixed-income project, High Point, that stands out as an entire green community, with its high old trees identified by community youngsters and then protected, creative plantings, a thriving community garden, sidewalks and streets tied into a "natural" water drainage system, and new energy-efficient condos and townhomes.

Out across the nation, there's fast-growing demand for public transit to save energy and transit-oriented development to curb sprawl. The move for major regional rail systems has now reached far beyond New York and Chicago, Boston and San Francisco to traditionally auto-dependent cities like Dallas, Denver, Salt Lake City, Phoenix, Albuquerque, Houston, and even Los Angeles.

Terminal Consumption?

Yet however welcome, even startling, the new developments seem, the somber truth is that the great ocean liner U.S.S. Consumption has so far shifted its direction barely a degree. With 4.6 percent of the world's population, the United States continues to burn a quarter of the globe's fossil fuels and to emit 25 percent of its greenhouse gases. Carbon dioxide emissions continue to climb and power companies claim a need to build 150 new coal-burning plants to slake our electric power thirst. Bigger and bigger houses, SUV road and gas hogs, vehicles for all members of the family, massive freeways and proposals for even greater ones, new gadgets by the dozens, near-lethal sugar and fat content of fast-food fare, the right to bloat our bodies and then count on the medical machine to fix them—we seem to want, and expect, it all.

And dwarfing campaigns for green values, the public is constantly exposed to the advertising budgets of GM, Ford, Wal-Mart, Pfizer, McDonald's, and the like—many billions of dollars a year, outweighing, by a factor of hundreds, efforts to educate Americans to a more conserving lifestyle.

Single-occupant auto commuting continues to grow, and carpooling and walking keep declining. Notwithstanding the decade-long push for "smart-growth" policies to protect the natural watersheds, the open fields and forests around our towns and cities, any check of existing zoning around the nation shows immense tracts of land zoned for added development. "You can't deal with sustainability [and] climate change if we insist on covering our open lands with one-, two-, three-acre house plots," notes Robert Yaro, president of the New York-area Regional Plan Association.

It's possible, if not likely, that carbon caps, monster storms, and global oil emergencies will soon alter the status quo more rapidly than anyone today imagines. Green has to be the future, many of its advocates argue, because in a resource-short and turbulent world, the American consumption lifestyle of the last 60 years will prove itself simply unsustainable.

In the meantime, the very best hope undoubtedly lies in the growing numbers of citizen groups and elected local officials who sense the changing world around them and have led today's remarkably broad search for fresh, new, green approaches.

Along the way, there are steps that could make an immense difference. One is a focus on the other green—money. We are beginning to see the dramatic, long-term savings that can be realized from green buildings and their reduced operating costs and increased property value. There's growing market acceptance of new green product lines, combined with the rapid growth of new clean technology funds. Green neighborhood and city planning, green water and power systems are on the rise. As a green economy emerges and proves its staying power, the momentum toward change will surely rise.

Health awareness should help too—demonstrating to the public the dramatic health benefits of green approaches and lifestyle, overcoming misleading, potentially disease-dealing advertising.

Government codes and regulations are another promising field for reform. Many of today's zoning and land-use regulations, building codes, and rules were written in response to public health and safety issues of a century ago, from tenement buildings without running water to slaughterhouses invading residential neighborhoods. Today we're stuck with sterile zoning and restrictions on building materials and methods alarmingly out of sync with present-day needs. A concerted effort by state and local governments to untangle obsolete building codes and set straightforward new standards, and to revamp outmoded zoning with modern and more flexible codes, could give a strong boost to the emerging green revolution. For example, zoning of the post–World War II era encourages "pods" of development—residential, office, and retail. The result is multiple auto trips that mitigate against compact, mixed-use, energy-efficient development.

Then there's the challenge to the professionals—the architects, planners, designers, engineers, builders, utility representatives, city and county housing officials, and others engaged on the front line of building and reshaping communities. Historically—and often, still today—they have worked sequentially, first doing the land planning, then the underground pipes, then roadways and buildings and so on.

In a smart 21st century, that won't do. It costs too much and it misses opportunities for better aesthetics, energy efficiency, and quality of life. The time's at hand to move from silos to systems. It's the right moment to ask the professionals to start thinking more broadly, to work closely with colleagues from the other disciplines from start to end of any project.

Green value sounds and is environmental. But it's so much more. It also stands for connectivity, intelligence, smart systems, and creating a 21st-century world that has a chance of being truly sustainable.

> *"Smart growth is . . . proving to be even more disastrous than the effects of the urban renewal programs of the 1950s and 1960s."*

Smart-Growth Policies Will Harm Urban Areas

Randal O'Toole

Randal O'Toole is a senior fellow at the Cato Institute and author of The Best-Laid Plans: How Government Planning Harms Your Quality of Life, Your Pocketbook, and Your Future. *In the following viewpoint excerpted from that book, O'Toole asserts that the dominant, coercive movement of smart growth—compact, pedestrian- and transit-oriented development—is neither desirable to most Americans nor a solution to traffic congestion. According to him, the population growth of suburbs exponentially outpaces that of downtowns, reflecting an overwhelming preference for suburban living. In addition, O'Toole argues that job concentration in downtown areas, not population density, encourages the use of public transportation, which smart-growth planners fail to recognize.*

Randal O'Toole, "When Government Plans, It Usually Fails," The Cato Institute, December 27, 2007. Copyright © 2007 Randal OToole. Used by permission of the author. October 19, 2010. www.cato.org/pub_display.php?pub_id=8868.

As you read, consider the following questions:

1. What numbers does O'Toole provide to show that most Americans do not desire to live in smart-growth neighborhoods?

2. What factors set the stage for the anti-sprawl movement, in O'Toole's view?

3. How does the author support his claim that proximity to work is not a high priority for most Americans?

Urban planners in Portland [Oregon] and many other cities today base their plans on a belief that Americans are too *auto dependent*, and that we have become that way as a result of land-use patterns that force people to drive and discourage transit, walking, and cycling. *Smart growth* is a land-use and transportation planning concept that calls for higher-density, compact urban areas, mixing commercial with residential uses, and emphasizing pedestrian-friendly design and transit-oriented development over automobile-oriented development, all aimed at reducing the amount of driving people need to do.

The term "smart growth" was first used in this way by Maryland Governor Parris Glendening in 1996. As one of Glendening's staff members later admitted, "The name 'Smart Growth' represented one of the Glendening Administration's smartest strategies," because it was "hard to oppose": anyone who questioned smart growth could be (and usually was) immediately accused of favoring "dumb growth." The clear implication is that anyone who wants to allow people to live the way that a majority of Americans actually do live must be dumb.

Before 1996, the concepts known as smart growth were often referred to as New Urbanism. Since then, at least some of the New Urbanists have distinguished themselves from smart growth by saying that smart growth is coercive, whereas New

Urbanists simply want to relax existing zoning codes so they can build for those people who would prefer to live in New Urban communities. Although few object to building New Urban projects where there is market demand, many smart-growth advocates want to use coercive policies to shape people's transportation choices.

A major problem with smart growth is that its advocates have badly mistaken the causal relationships that lead people to drive rather than walk or ride transit. Smart growth is based on the design fallacy, the idea that urban design shapes human behavior. In fact, the design features that smart growth would impose on urban areas have little effect on people's travel habits. They do, however, have significant negative effects on such things as congestion and housing prices.

Downtown Is Back?

[Sociologist] Herbert Gans pointed out that few middle-class families with children want to live in dense, lively neighborhoods such as [activist] Jane Jacobs's Greenwich Village. But in a typical planner fashion, smart-growth advocates reason that since most residents of dense, mixed-use neighborhoods are childless, therefore most child-free households will be glad to live in such neighborhoods. ([The logical fallacy can be expressed as:] "All dogs have four legs, so anything with four legs is a dog.") They imagine, for example, that as baby boomers become empty nesters, large numbers of them will want to move back to the high-density neighborhoods they enjoyed before they had children.

There is no doubt that some people prefer living in high-density, mixed-use neighborhoods. As Gans hints, they are mainly young singles or childless couples. But between 1990 and 2000, the vast majority of growth of these groups—in fact, in virtually every population group—was in the suburbs, not in cities.

163

Claims for a recent "downtown rebound" based on changing preferences toward high-density, mixed-use housing, for example, are greatly exaggerated. "'Downtown is Back' seemed to be a common observation in the 1990s," says a [mortgage provider] Fannie Mae study. "This was more than wishful thinking," the study says optimistically, but then adds, "The actual numbers of downtown growth are relatively small."

That's putting it mildly. The study looked at 24 urban areas and found that, during the 1990s, downtown populations had grown in 18 of them. But total population growth in those 18 downtowns was just over 54,000 people, an average of about 3,000 per downtown. During the same period, the cities surrounding those downtowns grew by more than 77,000 people and the suburbs of those cities grew by 5.54 million people, or more than 100 times as much as the downtowns. Considering that at least some of the cities in the study, including Denver and Portland, subsidized their downtown population growth, it is hard to see in these numbers much of a signal that Americans desire to live in smart-growth neighborhoods. . . .

A One-Way Street

The fundamental premise of smart growth—that urban design can and should be used to change people's transportation choices—is based on a misunderstanding about cause and effect. Smart-growth planners correctly recognize that there is a connection between transportation and land use; but they fail to accept that it is a one-way street: transportation technology influences land use, but land use does not significantly affect people's transportation choices. . . .

Steam trains in the 1830s, horsecars in the 1850s, cable cars in the 1870s, electric streetcars and subways in the 1890s, and automobiles in the 1910s each reduced transportation costs and allowed more people to live in their preferred styles of housing. For many, that meant a single-family home with a yard. While early technologies such as steam trains and horsecars were accessible only to the wealthy, electric streetcars helped create a growing middle class while Henry Ford's automobiles were affordable to the working class.

By the 1920s, the suburbs were fast becoming the dominant lifestyle, not only in America but in many other countries as well. "In the days of electrical transmission, the automobile and the telephone," said [architect] Frank Lloyd Wright in 1922, urban concentration "becomes needless congestion—it is a curse." "Cities are doomed," agreed Henry Ford in the same year. "There is no city now existing that would be rebuilt as it is, if it were destroyed." Ford was right: where early-19th-century cities had high population densities with concentrated job centers—think Brooklyn—late-20th-century cities have low population densities with widely dispersed jobs—think Phoenix.

While the Depression and World War II put a damper on suburbanization, it greatly accelerated after 1945. Between the 1950 and 1990 censuses, many major cities lost population while the overall urban areas in which they were located grew. The 2000 census revealed that some—though far from all—cities made a slight recovery, but in most cases their suburbs continued to grow far faster than the cities. . . .

Demonizing the Suburbs

While it doesn't threaten rural open space, health, or community, suburbanization did cause a number of feuds that set the stage for the modern anti-sprawl movement. Central city officials resented the suburbanites who seemed to take advantage of the city without paying their fair share of taxes toward it. Downtown property owners resented suburban shopping malls that quickly captured most of their retail business and suburban office and industrial parks that left some downtowns nearly vacant. Neighborhood residents resented the highways that took many homes and imposed noise and traffic on the homes that were left behind. Although most of the leaders of these groups lived in their own single-family homes with large yards, their solution was to demonize the suburbs and anyone who wanted to live in them.

For most people, automobiles provided access to low-cost land where they could afford to own their own homes. Far from causing congestion, the resulting low-density development was actually the solution to congestion. "Suburbanization has been the dominant and successful mechanism for coping with congestion," say University of Southern California planning professors Peter Gordon and Harry Richardson. People in suburbs don't necessarily want to drive more than people in cities. But because the suburbs are less congested, driving costs less, and so they may in fact drive a little more. At the same time, the growth of driving in dense cities has matched and in some cases exceeded driving growth in the suburbs.

A Weak Link

If traffic is the problem, then smart growth is entirely the wrong solution. The notion that higher densities lead people to drive less appeals to planners who suffer from the design fallacy, yet there is no merit to this belief. In 1999, a U.S. Department of Transportation researcher reviewed numerous studies on the relationship between density and driving. He found that those who claimed that density reduced driving were "spurious" because they failed to account for differences in such factors as income and household size. When such factors are considered, changes in driving are significant only at very high densities. For example, one study found that increasing suburban densities (1,000 to 2,000 people per square mile) to 25,000 or more people per square mile would reduce driving by only 11 to 25 percent. Another found that increasing densities from 3,600 people per square mile (the average for U.S. urban areas in 1990) to 5,400 people per square mile would reduce driving by less than 3 percent.

The weak link between density and driving can be seen in ... data from the 2000 census on how people usually traveled to work with population densities in the nation's 452 urban areas. In the vast majority of regions, more than 90 percent of commuters take autos to work. This group ranges from Kingsport, Tennessee, with a density of less than 1,000 people per square mile and where 98.5 percent of people drive to work, to Los Angeles, the nation's densest urban area at more than 7,000 people per square mile and where 91.5 percent of people drive to work. If density is a factor at all in these urban areas, it appears that multiplying density by seven times will get little more than 7 percent of commuters out of their cars.

Fewer than 90 percent of commuters choose to drive to work in just 49 of the 452 urban areas measured in the 2000 census. The 49 exceptions are almost all university towns or cities with major job centers in pedestrian-oriented downtowns. The university towns, including Davis, California; Ithaca, New York; and State College, Pennsylvania, have large percentages of young people who walk or bicycle to work. The major cities with large concentrations of downtown jobs, such as Boston, New York, and San Francisco, have many commuters who take transit to those jobs.

Job Distribution and Concentration

Unless planners outlaw middle age, they are unlikely to have much of an influence on the age distribution of individual urban areas. So the best opportunity they have to reduce auto commuting is by influencing the job distribution. Yet job distributions are influenced more by history than by government planning or regulation. American cities were built in three periods:

- Before 1890, cities were designed for pedestrians because few people could afford to travel except on foot. They had highly concentrated populations close to or intermingled with highly concentrated jobs.

- Between 1890 and 1930, streetcars were a dominant form of travel, especially for the middle class. Cities built during this period tended to have dense residential areas of single-family homes on small lots, but they were not necessarily close to the jobs. Jobs also spread out a little more and could be located in multiple centers instead of just downtown.

- After World War II, the automobile was the dominant form of travel. Cities built during this period tended to have low-density residential areas of single-family homes on large lots, and jobs were widely distributed throughout the area. These cities often lacked traditional downtowns unless the city had gone out of its way to subsidize high-rise construction.

Today, the only American cities with significant remnants of the pedestrian era are Boston, Chicago, New York, Philadelphia, San Francisco, and Washington. These urban areas still have concentrated job cores and a dense central-city population, surrounded by younger, lower-density suburbs. Most other cities that had been densely built before 1890 lost so much of their populations to the suburbs after 1945 that they no longer qualify as pedestrian cities. St. Louis, a once-dense city that lost 60 percent of its population to its suburbs after 1950, is a classic example.

The remnants of a classic streetcar city—a dense city of single-family homes—can be found today in much of Los Angeles. Many other northern cities such as Cincinnati, Minneapolis, and Seattle retain significant characteristics of the streetcar era. These urban areas have multiple job centers, but their population densities are much higher than the densities of their suburbs.

Many cities that have grown since World War II have virtually no characteristics of pedestrian or streetcar cities. They include Atlanta, Houston, and other Sun Belt cities that did not really start growing until air conditioning became affordable. These regions tend to have low densities and numerous job centers, and the central cities are often no denser than the suburbs. . . .

Las Vegas, Miami, and San Jose have greatly increased their densities in the past two or three decades, yet with both populations and jobs evenly spread out, transit plays a minimal role in commuting and travel. The overall densities of Boston, Philadelphia, and Washington are low, but with dense concentrations of jobs and people at their cores, transit plays a much larger role in commuting than in regions with denser populations but no significant job concentrations.

These numbers tell us that job concentration, not overall population density, is the key to making transit work. Even if the overall population density is low, it helps if a dense central city is located next to the concentrated jobs. This is confirmed by research in Montreal, one of the densest cities in Canada. "Denser areas have lower [per capita] auto ownership," the research found. "But it takes a large increase in density to reduce the number of vehicles a household owns." Moreover, because "people who don't want to drive are likely to choose locations where they don't have to," merely increasing population density won't reduce driving. The most important influence on reducing car ownership was "having a central-business district worker in the household." Overall, "centrality [of jobs] has more effect [on auto ownership] than population density."

A Mobile Society

Despite this, smart-growth planners do not call for concentrating jobs downtown. Instead, they seek a "jobs-housing balance" so that every part of an urban area has enough jobs to meet the needs of the residents of that portion of the area. This way, planners hope, people will live close enough to their jobs that they can walk or cycle to them. The problem is that, in a mobile society, people no longer consider proximity to work a high priority when locating their homes. In fact, one

University of California study found that people actually prefer to live some distance from work. So it is not surprising that University of California planning professor Robert Cervero found that jobs and housing in many San Francisco Bay Area communities "are nearly perfectly balanced, yet fewer than a third of their workers reside locally, and even smaller shares of residents work locally."

Smart growth is based on fundamental misunderstandings of how people, cities, and urban areas work. Yet it has become a dominant paradigm in many cities and regions that rely on urban planners to help them prepare for their futures. The results are proving to be even more disastrous than the effects of the urban renewal programs of the 1950s and 1960s.

> "The right-sizing agenda can be a foun-
> dation for [urban] rebirth, but must
> exude good planning."

Downsizing Large Cities Can Be Beneficial

Brian J. Connolly

A professional urban planner, Brian J. Connolly holds a master's degree in regional planning and a bachelor's degree in urban and regional studies from Cornell University. In the following viewpoint, Connolly argues that planned shrinkage—eliminating services and infrastructure in abandoned locations—can revital-ize Detroit. Many buildings in its neighborhoods, the author claims, are unsafe or unfit for preservation efforts, lacking prox-imity to economic activity or a strong real estate market. Thus, he advocates a planned-shrinkage strategy that is comprehensive, downsizes vacant infrastructure, hones in on concentrated growth and redevelopment, and involves suburban communities as a way of revitalizing slumping urban areas.

As you read, consider the following questions:

1. How should the zoning ordinance change in Detroit, in Connolly's opinion?

Brian J. Connolly, "Right-Sizing Done Right: How Planned Shrinkage Can Save Detroit," *Planetizen*, April 22, 2010. Reproduced by permission.

2. What developments should Detroit avoid, in the author's view?

3. What did the recession reveal about Detroit, according to Connolly?

Surrounding the intersection of Chene Street and Warren Avenue in Detroit are blocks of urban prairie, a wasteland devoid of people and dotted by abandoned buildings. One would be hard-pressed to believe that this spot is three miles from the downtown of America's eleventh-largest city.

Areas like these are the subject of Mayor Dave Bing's plan to "right-size" Detroit, cutting infrastructure and services to the most blighted areas. By shrinking Detroit, Bing rightly recognizes opportunities for the city to save resources and focus development efforts in healthier areas such as Midtown and Cass Corridor, the riverfront and other revitalizing neighborhoods.

Earlier this week [in April 2010] on Planetizen, [journalist and urban affairs commentator] Roberta Brandes Gratz rebuked the idea of shrinkage, arguing that a successful revitalization is built on preservation efforts. Gratz ignores Detroit's exceptional problems—no city has experienced the magnitude of abandonment that Detroit has, and no market exists to bring the city back.

Unlike neighborhood-decimating urban renewal, Detroit's right-sizing program targets areas that have neither people nor intact buildings. Preservation is important but in many Detroit neighborhoods, remaining buildings are too burned-out or unsafe for rehabilitation.

Preservation-based regeneration examples such as George-town [in Washington, DC], Harlem [in New York City] or neighborhoods in Brooklyn are not replicable in parts of Detroit. Some Detroit neighborhoods simply have nothing left to revitalize. Georgetown's regeneration was supported by its proximity to the nation's biggest employer, the federal government, and a large private university. Harlem's and Brooklyn's location in the New York real estate market was a key factor in their rebirth. Detroit has neither of these conditions.

Density is necessary, which is all the more reason Detroit must shrink. Detroit was always a low-density city. Closing vacant neighborhoods increases density by concentrating development in more limited areas.

To make right-sizing successful, Bing should integrate the program into a broader initiative with four elements.

Plan Comprehensively

First, instead of a piecemeal approach, right-sizing should be part of a citywide comprehensive planning effort. As portions of the city are closed down, stakeholders should be engaged to determine what a shrunken Detroit should look like.

An asset inventory would ground the effort in the city's strengths and direct the planning process. Afterward, updates to Detroit's outdated zoning ordinance would codify the city's goals, especially for closed-down areas, and could create a walkable and transit-oriented character for remaining neighborhoods.

Detroit has help available and models to follow. Recent national media coverage has planners itching to get involved, while philanthropic organizations stand ready to fund revitalization efforts. Local universities can contribute no-cost planning talent and generate ideas. Planning efforts in other large American cities, such as New York's PlaNYC program, can serve as models for a citywide planning effort.

Downsize Infrastructure

Second, although Bing's right-sizing strategy focuses on huge vacant areas, even Detroit's vibrant neighborhoods need infrastructure downsizing.

Midtown, one of the city's redeveloping neighborhoods, is an example. Its nine-lane-wide spine, Woodward Avenue, was

Internal Resettlement

If the city is to survive with a smaller population, the population must be encouraged to concentrate itself in the sections that remain alive. This sort of internal resettlement—the natural flow out of the areas that have lost general attraction—must be encouraged. The role of the city planner is not to originate the trend of abandonment but to observe and use it so that public investment will be hoarded for those areas where it will sustain life.

Roger Starr, New York Times Magazine, *November 14, 1976.*

outmoded in the 1960s by the construction of parallel freeways. Cutting vehicular lanes, offering transit options and adding pedestrian amenities would create an environment that encourages people to do more than drive through the neighborhood as well as improve pedestrian safety. Increased human activity would reduce crime, too.

Infrastructure right-sizing would reduce maintenance costs and build a more human scale, triggering investment. The successful rehabilitation of the downtown portions of Woodward, Broadway and Washington Boulevard in the early 2000s with landscaping and pedestrian amenities brought new development to the surrounding neighborhood and could be replicated elsewhere.

Focus Growth

Third, the right-sizing program should remain committed to targeted growth opportunities.

Detroit should rekindle momentum on initiatives such as riverfront redevelopment, facade improvements and streetscaping. The past decade saw over $1 billion in private investment

175

go into downtown and riverfront projects, and these efforts should not be wasted. With its strong nonprofit sector, the city can build on these successes and pursue development projects for key sites, particularly downtown. An inventory of vacant properties would start this effort.

Additionally, good physical development breeds successful revitalization efforts. Detroit can avoid desperate approaches to development that produce strip malls, gated communities and monolithic office complexes. The city should foster positive relationships with developers through collaborative efforts that ensure high-quality design and construction that foster an urban character instead of the suburban character typical of some recent projects.

Moreover, Detroit should pursue some landmark developments to catalyze neighborhood revitalization. The city should tear down or restore eyesores such as the Michigan Central Depot and the derelict Packard plant. Seeking creative redevelopment options, such as conversion of the Depot into a convention center or other public use would symbolically reestablish the city's control over its destiny.

Engage the Suburbs

Finally, the right-sizing plan presents a unique opportunity to engage the suburbs in a long-overdue regional dialogue. Detroit is not alone in its plight. The inner-ring suburbs have experienced abandonment and are in worse fiscal predicaments. The recent recession has exposed the whole region's overabundance of commercial and industrial space, and residential vacancies have crept higher even in outer suburbs. This shared reality should be addressed by the entire region.

Bing, a former sports star, businessman and quasi-suburbanite, is the best-positioned mayor in the city's history to reach beyond its borders. A City Council with new, young faces should open the doors to collaboration. Convincing arguments can make suburban leaders understand why Detroit's revitalization is of regional importance. Public education and media exposure are essential throughout the process.

Detroit is at a crossroads to which no city of its size has ever come, yet opportunity is knocking. The right-sizing agenda can be a foundation for rebirth, but must exude good planning.

In Bing, Detroit finally has a mayor who recognizes the city's reality and has the gravitas to build consensus. A strong nonprofit sector and philanthropic organizations are committed partners. The national media has taken interest in the city's redevelopment. Widespread interest in walkability, transit-oriented development and environmental sustainability can direct planning efforts toward high-quality development. By shrinking the city to a manageable size, the mayor might finally create a brighter future in Detroit.

| "Demolishing buildings does not solve
| social problems. It just displaces them
| to another locale."

Downsizing Large Cities Is Harmful

Roberta Brandes Gratz

Roberta Brandes Gratz is a journalist, urban affairs commentator, and author of The Battle for Gotham: New York in the Shadow of Robert Moses and Jane Jacobs. *In the following viewpoint, Gratz argues that cutting off services and demolishing buildings, or planned shrinkage, destroys the urban fabric of cities and displaces residents and businesses. Instead, she insists that rehabilitating and reoccupying distressed neighborhoods is an opportunity to address the housing crisis and allow people of all incomes to live in thriving metropolitan areas. In fact, local and grassroots efforts have transformed abandoned and formerly industrial areas into desirable communities, Gratz contends.*

As you read, consider the following questions:

1. What is the current state of cities, in the author's words?

2. Why should older buildings not be too-quickly deemed uninhabitable, in Gratz's view?

Roberta Brandes Gratz, "The Vacant-Building Syndrome," *Next American City*, Spring 2007. Reproduced by permission of the author.

3. What is the Soho syndrome, according to the author?

Demolition as a planning tool is back in vogue. Not since the discredited postwar urban renewal policies of the 1970s have political leaders embraced so wholeheartedly the idea of bulldozing vast [tracts] of vacant residential structures—and consequently, demolishing existing urban fabric, undermining local initiative, derailing organic regeneration, and displacing longtime residents and local businesses. When no productive policy exists, demolition is the easiest way to look like the problem is being addressed. The vacant building syndrome is simply planning by default.

This state of affairs comes at just the time when many older, deteriorated neighborhoods offer the best opportunity for urban regeneration and the best resource for addressing the national affordable housing crisis. This is not the 1970s, when so many cities hit bottom and the urban exodus was in full swing. The tide has clearly turned. Cities are increasingly enjoying a renewed popularity among middle- and upper-income groups. Real estate values in historic neighborhoods are accelerating beyond property owners' wildest dreams. Artists and other members of the "creative class" are seeking out abandoned or underused industrial neighborhoods. People who can afford to do so are moving into less car-dependent neighborhoods, meaning the car-free life is beginning to replace the suburban dream of the 1950s through the '80s. The opportunity for people with limited income to seek the same urban lifestyle, however, disappears when low-income neighborhoods are bulldozed.

Yet demolition of vacant structures is widespread. Philadelphia exhibits the problem in its most severe form, with nearly 60,000 vacant parcels (the highest per capita in the country). Small investments have been made in reclamation efforts, but the bulk of budgeted money is going for further demolition. Last fall [2006], the city of Buffalo, New York, said it planned to tear down a record number of vacant buildings in the 2006 fiscal year, around 1,000 deteriorated properties, nearly three times higher than the average number of annual demolitions since 2002.

Demolition Worsens Problems

The total number of vacant structures in the country is unclear. (According to the Brookings Institution, there have been no comprehensive, systematic assessments of the total number of abandoned buildings in more than a quarter-century.) But what is clear is that vacant buildings are often declared irredeemable too quickly. The basic quality of many older vacant structures is often higher than anything new built today. Most cleared sites, moreover, remain vacant for years, accelerating the deterioration of border, marginal communities and exacerbating the affordable housing shortage in almost every American city.

The politically saleable rationale for aggressive demolition is that drug addicts illegally occupy vacant buildings, which then become a scourge on their neighborhoods. Despairing neighbors can be the strongest constituency for demolition when they think no alternative exists. But demolishing buildings does not solve social problems. It just displaces them to another locale.

East Liberty, once a thriving trolley-car suburb of Pittsburgh and home of such luminaries as Gene Kelly [a dancer, singer, and actor] and Billy Strayhorn [a jazz musician and composer], became a poster child for failed urban renewal tear-down-and-rebuild policies. The city's Urban Redevelopment Authority demolished thousands of homes and buildings in the '50s and '60s. Residents left, and crime rose. In 2001, East Liberty Development, Inc., a grassroots group, demolished vacant '60s-era low-density mistakes, taking down 1,000 units in high-rise public housing or suburban single-family houses, building 200 affordable and 256 market-rate, tight-knit urban houses. At the same time, it started taking

Fallacious Reasoning

"Planned shrinkage" was based on fallacious reasoning and produced powerful consequences, both intended and unintended. It led to disinvestment in weaker neighborhoods and increased investment in what [urban critic Roberta Brandes] Gratz called "choicer" areas. As [New York City] neighborhoods like Harlem, the South Bronx, and Bedford Stuyvesant were burned, new construction—largely of middle-class and luxury housing—rose in such places as Roosevelt Island and Battery Park City. The decline in housing for the poor and working people of the city created a veritable "housing famine" that led to an epidemic of homelessness and a marked increase in the number of families living doubled- or tripled-up in the few remaining low-cost apartments.

Ichiro Kawachi and Lisa F. Berkman,
Neighborhoods and Health, *2003.*

possession of tax-delinquent vacant homes in the historic district adjacent to the commercial core, cleaning them out, patching the roofs, and boarding them up for future renovation. Fifteen vacant houses have been renovated and sold, with 30 more in the works.

"Vacant properties are the location of most of any area's crime," notes Ernie Hogan, East Liberty's Director of Residential Development, "but if you just demolish, the crime moves to the next easy place or it gets pushed onto the streets."

The Solution Is Local

The antidote to this sad state of urban affairs is positive reoccupancy—in other words, the small-scale reclamation of vacant housing by grassroots groups, followed by new infill of vacant lots. Community populations where this takes place wind up stabilized and ready for new infusions of people.

As far back as the 1970s, for example, Baltimore initiated a cutting-edge homesteading program that turned over city-owned properties to citizens committed to living in them for three years. The homesteader paid a nominal rent (usually $1 a year) and got a twenty-year, federally financed rehab loan at 3% interest. This was an early, if not the first, of the sweat-equity initiatives that revitalized many Baltimore neighborhoods, accomplished by the resident investors themselves. And yet today, instead of learning from the homesteading program, Mayor Martin O'Malley has chosen to replace redeemable urban housing with less-dense suburban housing, further eroding the city's urban fabric. On the western edge of downtown Baltimore, boarded-up rowhouses and vacant lots mark the edges of what was once the vibrant neighborhood of Poppleton. One of O'Malley's top priorities for this year [2007] is to demolish hundreds of these vacant homes to make way for a new $300 million community of single-family homes, townhouses, and apartments.

In Salt Lake City, three vacant buildings and one apartment house (150 units in total) were built in an abandoned industrial neighborhood, the Gateway District, paving the way for further upgrades and new construction. The result: a repopulated and growing mixed-income neighborhood with a new identity and name, the Artspace District, where experts thought demolition was the solution. "The few people who saw the potential and became champions over time were key," says artist Stephen Goldsmith. He and other artists needing cheap live-work space initiated the effort, joined by arts-related businesses and several non-profit users that now occupy the mixed-use buildings.

Almost every city that still has remnants of its industrial heritage contains SoHo-style conversions of warehouses and former manufacturing neighborhoods. This phenomenon—

the SoHo syndrome I call it in my book, *Cities Back from the Edge*—has gotten considerable attention because of its chic quality. But the same process is visible in modest-income neighborhoods. In Houston's Third Ward, artists, led by Rick Lowe, an Alabama-born painter and sculptor who moved to Houston more than two decades ago, started buying and upgrading derelict, vacant shotgun houses in 1990. The neighborhood of one-time tenant shacks built in the 1930s is now a vibrant downtown arts district confronting the reverse problem of gentrification.

An Old Problem

New York City was at rock bottom in the 1970s, losing 36,000 residential units a year over a decade; abandoned buildings seemed more plentiful than occupied ones. In 1976, the city's housing commissioner, Roger Starr, put forth a policy called Planned Shrinkage to address this seemingly intractable problem. The theory went like this: investing in neighborhoods where few people lived and restoring the old, deteriorating buildings there was a waste of limited resources. The city was shrinking, and so it made more sense to invest in populated neighborhoods with healthy commercial districts, letting the older neighborhoods die systematically. Today, this is called "Creative Shrinkage," and the model is Youngstown, Ohio, whose population dropped from a peak of 170,000 to 80,000 today. The plan calls for razing vacant buildings, cutting off sewage and electric service, and converting vacant land into pocket parks. According to a recent *New York Times* article, Youngstown's 35-year-old mayor, Jay Williams, has received many phone calls from other cities, asking how they can pursue similar plans.

When public officials advocated Planned Shrinkage in the '70s, the people remaining in these beleaguered communities resisted. In the South Bronx, a star example of local grassroots efforts, they occupied and renovated the abandoned buildings, turned rubble-strewn lots into parks, scraped together small grants and meagerly funded city programs, and began to re-build. Citizens chose to improve, rather than move, one building, one block, one neighborhood at a time. Wise city officials eventually recognized the momentum, accepted the challenge of local activists, and responded with innovative programs to support these local regeneration efforts.

Citizen efforts made areas in Northeast Philadelphia and downtown Detroit attractive to developers who, with generous financial incentives, built suburban-style housing and took credit for the renewal visible today. But organic urban neighborhoods are self-generated, not developer-built. "Lively, diverse, intense cities contain the seeds of their own regeneration," Jane Jacobs wrote 46 years ago in *Death and Life of Great American Cities*. This is true of troubled neighborhoods across America. Those seeds need the chance to germinate and flower, to be nurtured and fertilized, not plowed under and lost.

Periodical Bibliography

The following articles have been selected to supplement the diverse views presented in this chapter.

Drake Bennett	"How to Shrink a City," *Boston Globe*, September 5, 2010.
David Biello	"The Green Apple: How Can Cities Adapt to Climate Change?," *Scientific American*, June 16, 2010.
Nick Bjork	"In Oregon, a Stand Against Urban Renewal," *Portland Daily Journal of Commerce*, August 11, 2010.
Richard J. Dolesh	"Smart About Parks: The Smart Growth Movement Comes of Age with Help from Parks," *Parks & Recreation*, June 2010.
Roberta Brandes Gratz	"Shrinking Cities: Urban Renewal Revisited?," *Planetizen*, April 19, 2010.
Plaridel Inkana	"The Racist Gentrification of Our Cities," *IndyMedia*, December 21, 2009.
Joel Kotkin	"The War Against Suburbia," *American*, January 21, 2010.
Belinda Lanks and Kristi Cameron	"Greening the Urban Skyline," *Metropolis*, June 2010.
William S. Lind	"Love Your Neighborhood," *American Conservative*, June 16, 2008.
Lisa Rein	"Study Calls Md. Smart Growth a Flop," *Washington Post*, November 2, 2009.
Alex Taylor III	"A Michigan Success Story," *Fortune*, May 24, 2010.

For Further Discussion

Chapter 1

1. Steven Malanga claims that legislators behind the war on poverty believed that racism and globalization were too overwhelming to address on a local level. Does Barack Obama's plans for the crisis espouse this belief? Why or why not?

2. C.R. Sridhar maintains that the criminal theory of broken windows targets minorities and the poor. Do you agree or disagree with Sridhar? Cite examples from the viewpoints to support your answer.

3. Maco L. Faniel blames much of urban homelessness on institutional racism. Ian Merrifield suggests that addiction and mental disorders are primary causes of homelessness. In your opinion, who makes the more compelling argument? Use examples from the text to explain your response.

Chapter 2

1. Charles Woodyard asserts that mixed-income communities benefit public housing residents, but James Tracy contends that such developments displace such residents. In your view, who makes the more persuasive argument? Cite examples from the viewpoints to support your answer.

2. Todd Litman asserts that urban rail transit promotes economic development. Does Randal O'Toole successfully counter this assertion? Why or why not?

Chapter 3

1. Martha Yeide says city curfews can help direct high-risk teens to counseling and other services, and Tony Favro

agrees with her. Does Favro's agreement on this point, weaken his position against curfews? Why or why not?

2. Sharon Higgins and Caroline Grannan complain that charter schools exclude the neediest students. Monica Rohr describes a charter school with high-achieving underprivileged students. In your opinion, are charter schools helping poor students? Why or why not?

3. The Society for Research in Child Development states that several features must be present for a mentoring program to be effective. In your view, do the programs that Leslie Talmadge discusses possess these features? Use examples from the viewpoints to explain your response.

Chapter 4

1. Randal O'Toole argues that smart-growth planners are coercive. Do you believe the sustainable planning efforts discussed by Neal Peirce would be characterized as coercive? Cite examples from the viewpoints to support your answer.

2. Do you agree with Roberta Brandes Gratz that planned urban shrinkage displaces residents and businesses? Why or why not?

Organizations to Contact

The editors have compiled the following list of organizations concerned with the issues debated in this book. The descriptions are derived from materials provided by the organizations. All have publications or information available for interested readers. The list was compiled on the date of publication of the present volume; the information provided here may change. Be aware that many organizations take several weeks or longer to respond to inquiries, so allow as much time as possible.

Brookings Institution Metropolitan Policy Program
1775 Massachusetts Ave. NW, Washington, DC 20036
(202) 797-6000
e-mail: urbancenter@brookings.edu
website: www.brookings.edu

The Brookings Institution is an organization that researches and analyzes topics such as economics and governance. Its Metropolitan Policy Program provides decision makers with information about the challenges facing American cities. Publications available on the website include *The State of Metropolitan America* and *Metro Monitor*, its quarterly economic report on cities.

Cato Institute
1000 Massachusetts Ave. NW, Washington, DC 20001-5403
(202) 842-0200 • fax: (202) 842-3490
e-mail: cato@cato.org
website: www.cato.org

The Cato Institute is a libertarian public policy research foundation that aims to limit the role of government and protect civil liberties. Its website offers a number of publications on urban issues, including "The Myth of the Compact City: Why Compact Development Is Not the Way to Reduce Carbon Emissions" and "How Urban Planners Caused the Housing Bubble."

Congress for the New Urbanism (CNU)

140 S. Dearborn St., Suite 404, Chicago, IL 60603
(312) 551-7300 • fax: (312) 346-3323
e-mail: info@cnu.org
website: www.cnu.org

The Congress for the New Urbanism is a nonprofit organiza-. tion that teaches architects, developers, and others involved in the creation of cities the principles of New Urbanism. These principles include walkable neighborhoods and pleasant civic spaces. CNU's publications include newsletters, reports, and educational materials.

Employment Policies Institute

1090 Vermont Ave. NW, Suite 800, Washington, DC 20005
(202) 463-7650 • fax: (202) 463-7107
e-mail: info@epionline.org
website: www.epionline.org

The Employment Policies Institute is a research organization that studies issues affecting entry-level employment and employment growth. The institute, which sponsors research conducted by independent economists, opposes minimum-wage and living-wage policies. Publications available from the website include "Good Intentions Are Not Enough: Why Raising New York's Minimum Wage Continues to Be a Poor Way to Help the Working Poor."

Enterprise Community Partners, Inc.

10227 Wincopin Circle, Columbia, MD 21044
(800) 624-4298
website: www.enterprisecommunity.org

Enterprise Community Partners, Inc. (formerly the Enterprise Foundation) aids community developers by providing them with the tools they need to improve their cities, including consulting, training, and fund-raising support. Congressional testimony on issues such as housing can be found on the website, and other publications can be ordered.

National Coalition for the Homeless

2201 P St. NW, Washington, DC   20037
(202) 462-4822 • fax: (202) 462-4832
e-mail: info@nationalhomeless.org
website: www.nationalhomeless.org

The National Coalition for the Homeless uses public education, policy advocacy, and grassroots organizing to fulfill its goal of ending homelessness. Its work focuses on the areas of housing justice, economic justice, health-care justice, and civil and voting rights. Factsheets, reports, and information about legislation relating to the homeless are available on the website.

National League of Cities

1301 Pennsylvania Ave. NW, Suite 550
Washington, DC   20004
(202) 626-3000 • fax: (202) 626-3043
e-mail: info@nlc.org
website: www.nlc.org

The National League of Cities is an organization that represents municipal governments throughout the United States and aims to promote cities as centers of opportunity and leadership. Research briefs covering a variety of issues can be downloaded from the organization's website.

National Urban League

120 Wall St., New York, NY   10005
(212) 558-5300 • fax: (212) 344-5332
website: www.nul.org

The National Urban League is a community-based organization that helps African Americans improve their economic and social power. The league's publications include reports, studies, annual reports, and the *Opportunity Journal* and *Urban Influence Magazine*.

Poverty & Race Research Action Council (PRRAC)

1200 Eighteenth St. NW, #200, Washington, DC   20036
(202) 906-8023 • fax: (202) 842-2885
e-mail: info@prrac.org
website: www.prrac.org

The Poverty & Race Research Action Council is a not-for-profit organization whose mission is to create and distribute research about the relationship between race and poverty, promote policies that alleviate conditions caused by that relationship, and support social science research on those topics. PRRAC's newsletter *Poverty & Race* is published six times per year, and handbooks and anthologies can be ordered from the website.

Progressive Policy Institute

1730 Rhode Island Ave. NW, Suite 308
Washington, DC   20036
(202) 525-3926 • fax: (202) 525-3941
website: www.ppionline.org

The Progressive Policy Institute is a research and education institute that aims to define and promote new progressive politics for the United States. A variety of publications is available on the website, including policy briefings, reports, and articles about smart growth, transportation, and city politics.

Urban Institute

2100 M St. NW, Washington, DC   20037
(202) 833-7200
website: www.urban.org

The Urban Institute is a nonprofit educational and research organization that examines social, political, and economic problems. The institute also provides information to decision makers to help them address those issues. The website features publications on many urban issues, including crime, education, and welfare reform.

US Conference of Mayors
1620 Eye St. NW, Washington, DC   20006
(202) 293-7330 • fax: (202) 293-2352
e-mail: info@usmayors.org
website: www.usmayors.org

The US Conference of Mayors is the official nonpartisan organization of cities with populations of thirty thousand or more. Its roles include providing mayors with management tools, improving the relationship between federal and municipal governments, and creating a forum where mayors can exchange ideas. Press releases and webcasts are available on the organization's website.

Bibliography of Books

Elizabeth Blake   *No Child Left Behind? The True Story
                      of a Teacher's Quest.* Poughkeepsie,
                      NY: Hudson House, 2008.

Nicholas Dagen   *Public Housing That Worked: New
Bloom   York in the Twentieth Century.*
                      Philadelphia: University of
                      Pennsylvania Press, 2009.

Japonica   *The Gentrification Debates: A Reader.*
Brown-Sarancino   New York: Routledge, 2010.

Japonica   *A Neighborhood That Never Changes:
Brown-Sarancino   Gentrification, Social Preservation, and
                     the Search for Authenticity.* Chicago:
                     University of Chicago Press, 2009.

Abhijeet Chavan,   *Planetizen's Contemporary Debates in
Christian Peralta,   Urban Planning.* Washington, DC:
and Christopher   Island Press, 2007.
Steins, eds.

Henry G.   *From Despair to Hope: Hope VI and
Cisneros and Lora   the New Promise of Public Housing in
Engdahl   America's Cities.* Washington, DC:
                     Brookings Institution, 2009.

Wendell Cox   *War on the Dream: How Anti-sprawl
                     Policy Threatens the Quality of Life.*
                     New York: iUniverse, 2006.

Shawn A.   *Black Youth Rising: Activism and
Ginwright   Radical Healing in Urban America.*
                     New York: Teachers College Press,
                     2010.

William
Goldsmith and
Edward Blakely

Separate Cities: Poverty and Equality in U.S. Cities. Philadelphia: Temple University Press, 2010.

Roberta Brandes
Gratz

The Battle for Gotham: New York in the Shadow of Robert Moses and Jane Jacobs. New York: Nation Books, 2010.

D. Bradford Hunt

Blueprint for Disaster: The Unraveling of Chicago Public Housing. Chicago: University of Chicago Press, 2009.

Robert P. Inman,
ed.

Making Cities Work: Prospects and Policies for Urban America. Princeton, NJ: Princeton University Press, 2009.

Nikki Jones

Between Good and Ghetto: African American Girls and Inner City Violence. Piscataway, NJ: Rutgers University Press, 2010.

Joel Kotkin

The Next Hundred Million: America in 2050. New York: Penguin, 2010.

Cindy Ness

Why Girls Fight: Female Youth Violence in the Inner City. New York: New York University Press, 2010.

David Owen

Green Metropolis: Why Living Smaller, Living Closer, and Driving Less Are the Keys to Sustainability. New York: Riverhead Books, 2009.

Robert Pollin,
Mark Brenner,
Jeannette
Wicks-Lim, and
Stephanie Luce

A Measure of Fairness: The Economics of Living Wages and Minimum Wages in the United States. Ithaca, NY: Cornell University Press, 2008.

Robert C. Post — *Urban Mass Transit: The Life Story of a Technology*. Westport, CT: Greenwood, 2007.

Beryl Satter — *Family Properties: How the Struggle over Race and Real Estate Transformed Chicago and Urban America*. New York: Metropolitan Books, 2009.

Jack Stewart — *Graffiti Kings: New York City Mass Transit Art of the 1970s*. New York: Abrams, 2009.

Peter K.B. St. Jean — *Pockets of Crime: Broken Windows, Collective Efficacy, and the Criminal Point of View*. Chicago: University of Chicago Press, 2007.

Margery Austin Turner, Susan J. Popkin, and Lynette A. Rawlings — *Public Housing and the Legacy of Segregation*. Washington, DC: Urban Institute Press, 2008.

Sudhir Alladi Venkatesh — *Off the Books: The Underground Economy of the Urban Poor*. Cambridge, MA: Harvard University Press, 2009.

Edward Weiner — *Urban Transportation Planning in the United States: History, Policy, and Practice*. 3rd ed. New York: Springer, 2008.

James Wright — *Address Unknown: The Homeless in America*. Piscataway, NJ: Aldine Transaction, 2009.

Samuel Zipp   *Manhattan Projects: The Rise and Fall*
                     of Urban Renewal in Cold War New
                     York. New York: Oxford University
                     Press, 2010.

Sharon Zukin   *Naked City: The Death and Life of*
                     Authentic Urban Places. New York:
                     Oxford University Press, 2009.

Index